Iron Horse Imperialism

IRON HORSE IMPERIALISM

The Southern Pacific of Mexico, 1880–1951

DANIEL LEWIS

The University of Arizona Press   Tucson

The University of Arizona Press
© 2007 The Arizona Board of Regents
All rights reserved

First paperback printing 2008
ISBN 978-0-8165-2803-5 (pbk. : alk. paper)

LIBRARY OF CONGRESS CATALOGING-IN-PUBLICATION DATA
Lewis, Daniel, 1959–
Iron horse imperialism: the Southern Pacific of Mexico, 1880–1951
/ by Daniel Lewis.
p. cm.
Includes bibliographical references and index.
ISBN-13: 978-0-8165-2604-8 (hardcover : alk. paper)
ISBN-10: 0-8165-2604-4 (hardcover : alk. paper)
1. Ferrocarril Sud Pacífico de México—History.
2. Railroads—Mexico—History. I. Title.
HE2820.F38L48 2007
385.065′72—dc22   2006032951

Publication of this book is made possible in part by
the proceeds of a permanent endowment created with
the assistance of a Challenge Grant from the National
Endowment for the Humanities, a federal agency.

Manufactured in the United States of America on acid-
free, archival-quality paper containing a minimum of
30% post-consumer waste and processed chlorine free.

13 12 11 10 09 08   7 6 5 4 3 2

For my brand-new son

PAXTON JAY LEWIS

CONTENTS

ILLUSTRATIONS

The study of Mexican railroads remains a substantial hole in the historical scholarship of Mexico, the American West, transportation history, and border studies. This book, which began as a dissertation some eleven years ago, has benefited from the unveiling of new archival sources and new scholarship. Working as an archivist and curator responsible for the railroad and transportation materials at the Huntington Library provides me with a tremendous benefit—surrounded by some of the world's finest scholars from a variety of disciplines, I have had the advantage of both serendipitous and deliberate forays down many relevant roads.

A variety of sources in Mexico and the United States help to explore Mexico's treatment of the Southern Pacific of Mexico (SP de Mex; Ferrocarril Sud-Pacífico de México) and to address the questions posed herein. These sources include correspondence about regional issues, expressions of nationbuilding sentiments and attitudes, discussion of geographic issues affecting the line, and examples of the effects of diversity issues such as religion and race. They also reveal the complex and shifting attitudes of the Mexican government towards the railroad, and the collisions between the desires and actions of the government and the railroad.

Eight key sources examined consist of the Archivo General de la Nación (AGN) in Mexico City; the Archivo Histórico de la Secretaría de Relaciones Exteriores (AHSRE) in Mexico City; the Archivo de las Relaciones Extranjeros (ARE) in Mexico City; the Doheny Research

Foundation Records (DRFR) at Occidental College, Los Angeles, California; the corporate records of the SP de Mex at the Huntington Library (HLSPM) in San Marino, California; the José Maria Maytorena Collection at the Honnold Library (MCHL) at the Claremont Colleges in Claremont, California; a series of U.S. consular reports discussing Mexican railroad operations from the National Archives and Records Administration (NARA) in Washington, D.C.; and the Starr Papers at the University of California, Los Angeles (UCLA).

Some of the most important sources for this book came from Mexican archives. The AGN houses more than nine hundred separate files of correspondence that are in some way related to the SP de Mex, housed in the Department of Communications and Public Works (SCOP; Secretaría de Comunicaciones y Obras Públicas) collections. The AGN also holds correspondence between a number of Mexican officials and SP de Mex officials, including letters and telegrams between SP de Mex presidents and Mexican presidents Venustiano Carranza, Alvaro Obregón (1920–1924), Plutarco Elías Calles (1924–1928), Lázaro Cárdenas (1934–1940), and Avila Camacho (1940–1946). Legal issues, the wide gap between Mexican and U.S. perceptions of law and justice, and the heavily legally oriented nature of SP de Mex and Mexican dealings all played an important role in the SP de Mex's operations in Mexico, and these legal dealings in particular are addressed in the AGN material.

The second source, the AHSRE, includes a small but important series of correspondence about the SP de Mex. These materials deal with topics relevant to development of national identity, such as salary differentials between Mexican and non-Mexican workers, concerns about the presence of Mormon workers on the line, and other issues relevant to the tensions between the railroad and the government.

The third archival source is the ARE, a small but important collection of materials dealing with political and private foreign relations between Mexico and other countries.

The fourth archival source is the DRFR at Occidental College in Los Angeles. The DRFR is an uncataloged collection that includes typewritten reports and studies on all aspects of Mexican political, economic, and social life prior to 1917, generated by a team of experts sent to Mexico by oil tycoon Edward L. Doheny; it is housed in the Special Collections Department of the University Library.

The fifth source, the corporate records of the SP de Mex at the Huntington Library, consists of twenty-three boxes of unprocessed and unorganized material previously unavailable to researchers. This collection reveals much of the day-to-day operations of the company, including valuable information about Mexican perspectives in the form of correspondence from Mexican politicians and National Railways of Mexico's (NRM; Ferrocarriles Nacionales de México) personnel. The documents also include intracompany correspondence, financial records, detailed discussion of Mexican and U.S. legal and labor issues, communications about the effects of warfare on the line, including the Mexican Revolution and the Cristero Rebellion, and a variety of other material spanning the life of the railroad. Material from these papers, generated as they were by U.S. railroad officials, fleshes out the picture of the Southern Pacific Company (SP)'s middle management and its role within the larger parent corporation. A wide variety of other secondary and printed materials at the Huntington Library related to the history of the SP—detailed in the bibliography herein—has also proved tremendously helpful.

The sixth archival source is the José Maria Maytorena Collection at the Honnold Library at Claremont Colleges in Claremont, California. This collection consists of 2,200 letters to and from Maytorena (governor of Sonora, 1911–1914) between 1887 and the late 1920s. Correspondents include Porfirio Díaz, Bernardo Reyes, and other political elites of the day. Maytorena was a wealthy native Sonoran landowner who was active in state politics and had close friendships with Reyes and Reyes's son Rodolfo. Because it operated in the state of Sonora starting in 1881, well before the company expanded southward, the SP de Mex played an integral role in Sonoran life earlier than in the other states through which it later passed. The strength of this collection lies in the correspondents' awareness of the Sonoran region's distinctness and self-identity.

U.S. State Department consular reports make up the seventh major source. These reports contain abundant consular views of the SP de Mex and of other railroads and corporations operating in Mexico.

These reports provide an excellent window into the U.S. government's changing attitudes towards Mexico and towards the role of foreign capital in hemispheric relations. They reveal what most other U.S. government records pertaining to Mexico do not: the status of life within Mexico written by U.S. government officials living in the country. Alan Knight has called U.S. consular reports from Mexico "a magnificent source . . . for the history of foreign interests in Mexico . . . [and] still relatively unexploited" (Knight, *Mexican Revolution*, x). U.S. consular officials also had one important element in common with the administrators of the SP de Mex: they were in the country, but not of the country.

UCLA's Starr Papers provide the eighth primary source of material used to examine the railroad-government relationship. In particular, they deal with the ethnic and racial elements found in Sonora that collided with both railroad and government in the 1920s. These materials consist of correspondence, scrapbook clippings, and news items. UCLA's book and pamphlet collections, while not primary sources, also include a number of extremely rare printed materials of great value in understanding the dynamics of Mexican railroads.

I have organized this book so that it begins by illuminating Mexican government relations with the construction and growth of the country's railroad lines in general, again involving the elements noted above. In particular, chapters 1 and 2 analyze the attitudes, perceptions, and actions of the Mexican government in developing and managing its railroads under the umbrella of the NRM, the national railroad organization created in 1899. Chapter 3 then moves into an explicit study of relations between the SP de Mex and Mexican railroad administrators and government leaders, primarily during the Mexican Revolution. Chapter 4 studies this relationship between 1923–1929, including the period of final construction on the line through the Salsipuedes Gorge, and chapter 5 examines the web of ethnicity and otherness related to the railroad's operations during the same period, especially in Sonora. Chapter 6 scrutinizes the role of labor and the increasingly effective regulatory mechanisms put into play by the government between 1930 and 1939. Finally, chapter 7 discusses the inevitability of the railroad's decline and the historically conditioned factors driving both sides in the relationship.

As Richard Orsi has demonstrated in his recent groundbreaking work on the SP and the development of the American West, the story of the middle management of the SP—its broad central administrative core—has not heretofore been told in any detail (Orsi, *Sunset Limited*). The SP de México's officers and decision-makers fell squarely into this category: they acted as senior staff members of the subsidiary but served as mid-level functionaries within the larger SP, which devoted the lion's share of its energies to its far more financially successful and densely strung network of lines north of the U.S.–Mexico border.

ACKNOWLEDGMENTS

A number of colleagues and institutions helped in the birth of this book. I completed the dissertation just as I was starting a curatorial career at the Huntington Library in San Marino, California, in 1997. Colleagues, fellow scholars, and friends all informed the work. They are far too numerous to list in their entirety, and my apologies for any notable exclusions. Among the many scholars who have had useful comments and observations about my dissertation were Sam Truett of the University of New Mexico, Bill Deverell of the University of Southern California, Teresa M. Van Hoy of the University of Houston, Tom Sitton of the Los Angeles Natural History Museum, Walter Brem of the Bancroft Library, Dick Orsi of Cal State Hayward, and two terrific scholars of the American West now gone but never to be forgotten: Martin Ridge and Wilbur R. Jacobs. Donald Duke, the publisher of Golden West Books, also provided access to his unparalleled private library of railroadiana. Bill Wheaton created the map (fig. 1.1) in the book. My boss, colleague, and friend Mary Robertson offered unreasonable amounts of support in a variety of forms. Not only has she worked unstintingly for some thirty years to make the Huntington—through her scholarship and her stewardship of the collections—one of the world's great research libraries, but she has helped to make it one of the best places to work as a curator. I also owe a particular thanks to Peter Blodgett, the Huntington's Curator of Western Historical Manuscripts, whose warm friendship and gentle but steadfast encouragement have perhaps motivated me more than anything else to finish this project.

During the years of archival research on the book, I made extensive use of the Biblioteca Iberoamericana of the University of Guadalajara; the Archivo General de la Nación, Mexico City; and the Archivo Histórico de la Secretaría de Relaciones Exteriores, Mexico City.

At the University of California, Riverside, where the project began, my lodestar and greatest supporter was Carlos Cortés, my outstanding and rigorous advisor and committee chair, who has encouraged me from start to finish, along with my dissertation committee members Rob Patch and Devra Weber; examination committee members Ed Butler and Roger Ransom; Ron Chilcote; and Larry Burgess, who over the last two decades has variously served as mentor, professor, supervisor, and close friend.

My parents, Hal and June Lewis, and my brother, Gene, all of whom passed away during the course of this project, never wavered in their support and enthusiasm. Finally, my wife, Pamela Bailey Lewis, and our playpen of animals—Nutmeg, Hula, and Edgar—all provided nurturing, general hilarity, and all of the inducements to success on a substantial undertaking that one hopes for but rarely is so lucky to receive so abundantly.

Dan Lewis
Pasadena, California
April 2006

Iron Horse Imperialism

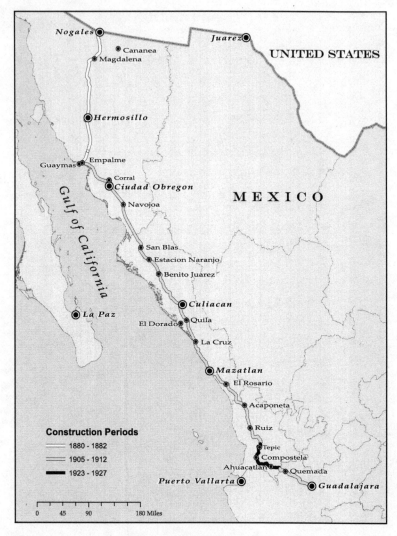

1.1 SP de Mex route from Nogales to Guadalajara, showing the three different periods of construction leading to the line's completion in 1927. (Courtesy of William D. Wheaton)

CHAPTER 1

Nationbuilding Versus Foreign Penetration

The Question of Why Southern Pacific of Mexico Operations Failed

"Things aren't so bad in the railroad operating business that they couldn't be worse," remarked Walter Douglas, the president of the Southern Pacific of Mexico (SP de Mex; Ferrocarril Sud-Pacífico de México), to U.S. reporters in 1938.[1] In a perverse way, Douglas was correct. Although the railroad had already fallen upon hard times in Mexico by 1938, its fortunes could and did get considerably worse in the years to come.

This book analyzes Mexico's treatment of the SP de Mex—a U.S.-owned railroad that operated in Mexico between 1898 and 1951, running from the Sonoran town of Nogales, just across the U.S.–Mexico border from Arizona, down to the city of Guadalajara, and stopping at a series of northwestern cities and port towns along the way. In the course of scrutinizing actions by Mexico, it also provides new insights into the ways in which U.S. companies and their foreign subsidiaries have interacted, often to the detriment of both.

The only railroad to ever operate regularly along the Mexican west coast, the line was owned by the Southern Pacific Company (SP) of the United States. It provided intranational passenger and freight service, as well as international service to and from the United States. The railroad offered central and southern Mexico a rapid and reliable link to the northwest for the first time. It transported millions of tons of freight and millions of passengers over the years, as well as serving as a strategic military tool for diverse factions in the Mexican Revolution and the Cristero Rebellion.

Strangely, however, despite providing this variety of services and opportunities to Mexico, the line became a constant frustration to the SP and, from the railroad's perspective, a failure in many ways. The company owned the line but could not control key aspects of its operations, nor attain the basic company goal of generating steady profits. Despite taking in substantial income from various sources, primarily freight and passenger revenue, the railroad hemorrhaged money throughout its half-century of operation. The SP never succeeded in turning a profit in Mexico, other than for two years following completion of the line in 1927 and for three years during World War II. And even those five years of profitability proved to be times of greatest duress for the company.

As we will see, one of the primary reasons for the railroad's stubborn continuation of operations in Mexico was that railroad executives' particular brand of imperialism—as well as urgings from the media—worked to keep the company committed to the railroad long after it made any business sense. Harking back to earlier motivational examples of U.S. conquest and subjugation of both land and peoples, both in its internal communiqués and in external publicity, the line was the subject of exhortations about the value of continuing during difficult times. As we will see, these refrains contributed to the railroad's continuation of their operations despite losing money year after year.

Another reason for the railroad's demise was Mexico's fundamentally different attitude towards other foreign companies. Mexican politicians provided far greater concessions to other foreign companies and a much more hospitable environment in which to do business. Government officials routinely allowed these enterprises to effectively regulate their own operations and to influence Mexican legislation and taxed them far less heavily. Corporations such as Standard Oil, the Pearson Trust, Wells Fargo, the United Fruit Company, Coca-Cola, and Sears, Roebuck & Co. had met with considerable success in Mexico. Why not the SP?

Other foreign businesses sometimes even received assistance from Mexico to a degree that muted Mexican sovereignty. For example, Mexico signed the Bucareli Agreements in 1923 as a direct concession to U.S. oil companies—even though the Obregón government seriously compromised the integrity of the 1917 Mexican Constitution by doing so. President Plutarco Elías Calles, elected a year later, then reinforced these agreements in late 1924 with another round of deals that further weakened Mexican sovereignty by allowing U.S. landholders to violate Article 27 of the Mexican Constitution. These new agreements gave subsoil rights to some private landholders rather than to the state.

The SP de Mex never received this brand of deferential treatment, despite the potential revenue and other advantages Mexico stood to gain from the completion of the railroad's line. (Although construction had been started southward from Guaymas in 1909, and commerce and passengers plied the two unconnected halves of the line from 1909 onward, the final 166-kilometer gap between Tepic and La Quemada was not completed until 1927, fully connecting northwestern Mexico to Guadalajara.) Finalization of the railroad meant that Mexico's railroad network was now truly geographically comprehensive, spanning the length and width of the country for the first time. But despite the advantages of finally having this linkage, Mexico considered the SP de Mex to be like a grain of sand in the oyster of the country: irritating at times, but tumescent with possible riches and advantages, and thus not worth spitting out altogether.

The company's hugely successful previous railroad experience in the United States makes its failures in Mexico a puzzle. With its corporate knowledge, money, experience, and ambition, and its large, experienced, powerful, and well-organized administrative and technical teams that had successfully navigated the shoals of fierce competition, onerous federal regulations, public wrath, difficult geography, and a wildly fluctuating economy in the United States, the SP had all the apparent prerequisites to flourish in Mexico. Yet it did not.

The reasons for this differential treatment and the railroad's failure were directly related. The changing ways in which Mexico treated the railroad reflected the government's evolving attitudes about the place of foreign railroad companies in the national transportation infrastructure, as well as an increasingly well-defined sense of nationhood. Riddled with contradictions during the Porfiriato, Mexican nationbuilding expressions and actions regarding the railroad eventually became more uniform, more logical, and more consistent over time. The 35-year Porfiriato, which lasted from Porfirio Díaz' ascension to power in 1876 until his exile in 1911, was an era marked by tremendous economic and financial growth for Mexico but marred by corruption and a lack of improvement in the living conditions for the vast majority of Mexicans.

Because the relationship between the parent company and its Mexican subsidiary played a critical role in the SP de Mex's failures and successes, the book also scrutinizes the parent SP's relationship with its Mexican line in considerable detail. New sources and information pertaining to the SP have come to light in the last several years, providing new contextual opportunities for a better understanding of the parent company as well as its Mexican line.

The settling of Europeans in Latin America created the first conflict of self-identity for the region: who were the true sons and daughters of the soil? The Spanish and Portuguese came to Latin America in the late fifteenth century as new and strange conquerors, terrifying to the native populations and full of alien ways. Over many years, however, Spanish and Portuguese bloodlines, animals, tools, religious beliefs, and other imports from the Iberian peninsula had mixed so widely with the native populations and African elements that these once-conquering imports had become as "American" as anything of pre-Columbian origin.

The railroads arrived in Latin America in the mid-nineteenth century in a similar way. They first appeared as foreign, almost otherworldly beasts, pushing and snorting their way across the countryside like iron horses. But as the decades passed, railroads began to become integral elements of national pride and self-identity for most countries in Latin America. In the process, they also influenced Latin American perceptions of travel, technology, industry, politics, and even human relations. The introduction of railroads owned by foreigners in large South American countries like Argentina and Brazil created a tension between their foreign owners and those within the country who maintained that the railroad was a more nationalistic element. It was a highly unequal relationship which meant that the needs of the country were subsumed to the needs of the foreign owners.

Mexico, however, managed its relationship with the foreign railroads differently. It worked to maintain and extend national integrity and self-identity in the face of both the promise and the threat of foreign corporate involvement in the country. The SP de Mex phenomenon was part of the larger picture of Mexico's nationbuilding efforts and tensions. Yet the railroad also received a particular form of treatment because of the exceptional size, wealth, and reputation of the parent corporation that owned and oversaw the railroad—the SP.

Mexican leaders had a variety of goals in their relationship with the railroad from its first days as the Sonora Railway up through its sale to the government in 1951. They wanted the line to provide important gains for the country: economic growth from intra- and international commerce along the west coast; military efficiencies; and transportation for passengers. But leaders also feared that the railroad could undermine Mexican sovereignty by dictating or influencing specific aspects of life in Mexico, including labor conditions, language, ease of military intervention from the north, and even religious direction. The SP de Mex presented the government with these challenges—ones that stemmed from the company's presence, wealth, persistence, and desires. Ultimately, the relationship provided politicians with the opportunity to fully confront the tensions and apparent contradictions of welcoming large doses of foreign capital and activity while simultaneously strengthening the country's economy and stabilizing its political structure.

In some ways, these issues reflected a larger struggle taking place throughout Latin America from the mid-nineteenth century until World War II: the relationship between foreign capital and Latin American governments. Latin American elites had taken up the debate strongly and vocally during this period. This debate centered on what contributions foreign capital should and could be allowed to provide towards the improvement and futures of individual nations. Other Latin American countries generally defined "improvement" in the same key ways as did Mexico: they desired to build their infrastructures (particularly transportation and communications aspects), shore up their economies, and better the working conditions and lives of their residents. But along with the promises and hopes of economic growth and the strengthening of infrastructure, potential and real threats also arose. Many leaders feared that foreign corporate involvement could facilitate military incursions by other countries, drain income from Latin America to other parts of the globe, and force countries to relinquish political or economic control to extranational corporations.

What were the particular tensions and issues at hand in the relationship between Mexico and the SP de Mex? Five primary elements stand out: the geographic proximity of the railroad to the U.S.–Mexico common border combined with its distance from central Mexico; questions and concerns about the company's own legal identity as either Mexican or U.S.; perceptions by Mexican and U.S. observers and participants of the railroad as a conqueror and penetrator; the evolving role of law defining the Mexican government–SP relationship; and Mexican treatment of the "otherness" of both the railroad and of the diverse ethnic and ideological factions intersecting with the railroad.

First, Mexico's location in the hemisphere provided a vital element in Mexican nationbuilding efforts and the country's relationship with the railroad. With the exceptions of Caribbean nations, all Latin American nations share borders with other countries. But only Mexico shares a border with the United States (fig. 1.2). This accident of geography made the case of Mexico unique in Latin American railroading. Northern Mexico, isolated and distant from the influence of central Mexico and lacking a large sedentary Indian population, developed without the same constraints that the federal government and the Catholic Church imposed on other areas of the country.

On the northern border, the state of Sonora has played a particularly important role in Mexican interactions with the railroad. As a frontier region, Sonora was isolated from the capital but stimulated and influenced directly by the more economically and politically powerful United States. Because a number of Mexican presidents during the life of the SP de Mex came from Sonora (including Alvaro

1.2 SP de Mex engine crossing the international border at Nogales, entering into Mexico from the United States. (Courtesy of Donald Duke, Golden West Books, San Marino, California)

Obregón and Calles), they often had business and family ties there, accompanied by vested interests in Sonoran projects and a desire to regulate or protect activities and commerce in the region. The railroad provided one means by which to influence activities in the region. But Sonora has also had a long history of rebelliousness against the central government and remained culturally and physically remote from central Mexico. Elements of religion, ethnicity, and race collided in the region and both affected and were affected by the SP de Mex. The dynamics of having the United States pressing up against a region that central Mexico had historically misunderstood, mistreated, or ignored, but over which Mexican leaders also desired to maintain control, played an important element in the government-railroad relationship.

The Sonora Railway was the only line in the region for many years, making it an integral part of the region's landscape. In the process, the railroad assumed an identity that caused it to appear as much Sonoran-owned as U.S.–owned. And the fact that the Sonoran region was alien to Mexico City in many ways influenced central government perceptions of the SP as a foreign element to be grappled with. An 1885 description by one Mexican writer of the region portrayed Sonora as a world unknown, wild and different and dangerous somehow: "The local geography appears to me to be changing; the ground is new, the tribes unknown, and they scarcely have notions of a civilized town that serves as the social key to one of the most important states in the Confederation . . . [the native populations] have created here a species of 'a state within a state' that is a constant threat to the society and government."[2]

The second element of the government-railroad relationship, briefly noted here but of critical importance because of when and how it appeared, was the issue of the line's legal identity as perceived by both Mexico and the railroad. A number of pragmatic advantages existed for companies that had juridical status as Mexican rather than foreign companies. The issue of the railroad's status as U.S. or Mexican was dictated by Mexican law and arose at critical junctures in the railroad's life. As Mexico increasingly dictated the conditions under which the railroad did business in the country, the SP de Mex became more and more desirous of changing its status from U.S. to Mexican for the advantages that would accrue. Both Mexico and the SP de Mex changed their views of the railroad's identity at times and acted accordingly. And although Mexican laws dictated which companies were Mexican and which were not, the laws, and their interpretations, changed as the years passed.

A third component defined the Mexico–SP relationship, and it was perhaps the most deep-seated, diffused, and vital of the five elements: conceptions by both U.S. corporate executives and Mexican politicians for many years of railroads as penetrators and conquerors. The conquest-laden attitudes of the SP in particular clashed against increasingly defensive attitudes and actions of the Mexican government to protect against these perceived attempts at conquest.

Railroads inherently seemed to contain elements conducive to the idea of conquest, penetration, and superiority. Works published out-side of Mexico at the time of the SP de Mex's incorporation empha-sized the idea of conquest over nature—and in particular, conquest over foreign lands. A 1911 book entitled *The Railway Conquest of the World* included chapters such as "The Romance of Construction" and noted that "no matter how formidable any obstruction may appear, it is the work of the builder to beat it down; to overcome it by some means or another with the minimum of expense. He must be baulked by nothing."[3] Other chapters emphasizing this idea of conquest in-cluded "The Railway Invasion of Canada" and "The Invasion of the Far East." For this author, and for others writing early in the twentieth century in the era of Teddy Roosevelt's Big Stick diplomacy, railways served as vehicles of penetration and incursion abroad.

The implication is clear, and the distance short, between two ideas: that of railroads conquering difficult terrain, and that of the railroad as a subduer of the peoples themselves inhabiting that terrain. The first notion had sharp edges and could be easily quantified: the busi-ness of construction was an engineering task. The second notion, though, proved considerably more vague. What did it mean to say that a railroad "conquered" a country? SP de Mex officials occasion-ally uttered sentiments about conquering and "Americanizing" the country. But lip service to the idea was not the critical element. The concept of conquest and the imperialism which accompanied it be-came central in the SP de Mex case because it probably drove the railroad's desires to complete and continue the line, long after doing so was practical.

These ideas of the railroad as a conqueror were held widely in Latin America. The doctrine of Positivism, the belief in the triumph of science and the scientific method, provided one of the clearest manifestations of these ideas of penetration and conquest within Latin America generally but was also particularly evident in Porfirian attitudes about railroads. One of the strongest desires of Latin Ameri-can elites, steeped in Positivist thought from Europe in the nineteenth century, was the desire for order—more specifically, the desire to conquer disorder, "backwardness," and underdevelopment. Railroads met these criteria because they included elements important to Positivists: technology, order, and progress. All of these qualities were necessary for the conquest of untamed regions. The railroad seemed like a solution of the highest degree to many Positivists in Latin America. The fact that vital elements of railroad operations were foreign—including technology imported from overseas, foreign capital to support the rapidly growing lines, and foreign workers to build and administer them—was secondary for many decades to the perceived benefits of the railroad.

In Mexico, during the last two decades of the Porfiriato, the *científicos*, a group of Positivist-, progress-, and technology-oriented men, gained increasing influence over politics, government and private presses, and educational policy. As Dirk Raat has pointed out, the subsequent dispersal of Positivist doctrine through the media and the schools gave shape to Positivism as an identifiable form of Mexican pride and strength.[4] This spread of Positivism among elites in Mexico was strong and persistent; more than fifty major scientific organizations produced a steady stream of journals, touting the benefits of systematic and controlled thought. These attitudes about Positivism would overshadow other Mexican attitudes about the value of imported technology and know-how until after the revolution.

Fourth came the role of law in the relationship: in particular, how Mexico used, and the SP de Mex responded to, legal mechanisms such as taxes, tariffs, and other assessments of fees. The government also used other legal controlling mechanisms such as the 1899 Railroad Law, the 1908 law forming the National Railways of Mexico (NRM; Ferrocarriles Nacionales de México), elements of the 1917 Mexican Constitution, and the Federal Labor Law of 1931. As these laws and the means used to enforce them evolved, they provided the government with a way to regulate the railroad and prevented the SP de Mex from exercising its own desires in a number of spheres.

The fifth and final element consists of the government's treatment of otherness—primarily how it responded to ethnic and ideological differences that intersected with the railroad. Conflicting elements within Mexico, especially in Sonora, further complicated and hindered several different kinds of relations with the railroad. National suspicion of Chinese, Mormon, and Yaqui laborers on the line as well as Yaqui depredations against the railroad led to further difficulties in effective and profitable shipment of goods and passengers along the line.

Groups in the country's northwest regions provided one source of otherness, but the railroad itself provided another important aspect. Outside of the umbrella of the national railway system and of foreign extraction, the railroad was viewed as both malevolent interloper and benevolent resident, depending on the circumstances at hand. The book thus also probes the reasons for, and methods of, the government's treatment of the railroad as a foreign or native object.

The relationship between Mexico and the United States contained a number of imbalances that brought the idea of the railroad as a conqueror of Mexico into even sharper relief and generated ongoing tensions in the Mexican government–SP de Mex relationship. Of the two neighboring countries, the United States had the greater wealth, political power, and technological development. But Mexico had something that the United States lacked—a visceral understanding of what it meant to lose large quantities of land to a more powerful neighbor. It also had motivations—arguably, compelling ones—to repulse the perceived "conquest" of the SP de Mex.

While the North American railroad behemoth had financial profit as its primary explicit goal, Mexico had its own objectives in the relationship—self-preservation of elements of national integrity, an opportunity to knit the entire country together by rail for the first time, and the strengthening of means for military dispersal and protection. It also had its own financial goals, including the boosting of national commerce and passenger traffic, as well as adding to federal coffers through the accumulation of taxes and other fees imposed on the railroad.

The SP de Mex's very size, wealth and visibility to Mexican politicians and observers renders it an excellent case study with which to analyze Mexican attitudes and defense mechanisms against foreign penetration, as well as the issues of power and control that have accompanied foreign corporations on their excursions into Latin America. Many in Latin America have argued that the acceptance of foreign capital on a large-scale amounts to *vendepatria* on the part of elites and other decision-makers in a position to interact with those foreign companies.

In studying the SP de Mex case, the book argues that the railroad was more than simply an element of U.S. corporate hegemony to be regulated by the government. The government was not just standing its ground against foreign economic, juridical, or cultural intrusion. The Mexican government was able to influence the line so that it actually contributed actively to Mexican nationbuilding. Mexico ultimately maintained control over the railroad's activities and blunted its ability to shape the course of Mexican events in such spheres as politics, finance, and law, while simultaneously benefiting from the building, completion, and operation of the line.

CHAPTER 2

"Ungrateful Yankees and the Means to Combat Them"

Mexican Governmental Treatment of Railroads
(1837–1920)

Mexican railroad history divides into five eras.[1] The first consisted of the extended period from first concession to actual completion of the country's first line between 1837 and 1880. The second involved the strong and steady railroad construction and the rapid influx of foreign capital from 1880 to 1911. Third came the rocky and contentious era from 1911 until the signing of the Bucareli Agreements in 1922. The signing of these agreements provided Mexico with a consolidated loan that paid off many of the debts from the Mexican Revolution, including most of the monies claimed by U.S. shareholders for damage to U.S. lines under the umbrella of the national railway system, the National Railways of Mexico (NRM; Ferrocarriles Nacionales de México). But in assuming the loan, the government generated new debt, this time to the U.S. bankers who had loaned Mexico the money. These loans generated a half-billion pesos of new debt for Mexico. Gradually but consistently evolving Mexican attitudes towards foreign railroads after 1922 marked the fourth era and eventually led to nationalization of almost all railroads in Mexico in 1938 by decree of President Lázaro Cárdenas. Finally, the fifth era has been the economic struggle of Mexican railroads from 1938 to the present, marked by strong and persistent labor agitation.

This chapter emphasizes the second and especially the third periods of 1880–1911 and 1911–1922. These years mark the most significant administrative and legal changes for Mexican railroads. They also mark the start of a long period of U.S. involvement in Mexican railroading and thus provide a wealth of examples of, and reactions to, the wave of foreign investment crashing upon the shore of Mexican desires for maintenance of national integrity. This forty-two-year period also includes the birth of three legal mechanisms affecting all railroads in Mexico: the 1899 Railroad Law; the 1908 creation of the NRM; and the 1917 Mexican Constitution, which had both immediate and long-term effects upon foreign railroads under the NRM umbrella as well as on the Southern Pacific of Mexico (SP de Mex; Ferrocarril Sud-Pacífico de México).

The course taken by Mexico's railroads has differed from that of other Latin American countries in three important ways. First, Mexico was one of the last two nations to develop railroads (only Chile took longer to inaugurate its first line, doing so in December 1873, just eleven months after Mexico). Because of this late start, Mexico gleaned through observation many of the lessons that other countries, notably Argentina and Brazil, had learned firsthand in their own earlier struggles to build viable railroad networks. Second, Mexico is the only Latin American country whose railroads connected with those of the United States because of the geographic accident of a common border.[2] Third, the struggle between foreign capital and Mexican political elites affected the country's railroads not just differently, but also produced more intensity and conflict than in any other Latin American country. Mexico's protracted efforts to build its first line illustrate the start of the country's long struggle over the nature of foreign capital and the role it should play in railroad expansion.

1837–1880: From Plan to Reality

Mexico's efforts to develop a railroad system between 1837 and 1880 reflect the turmoil the country endured after it emerged, blinking, into the harsh sunlight that followed independence from Spain in 1821. Railroads had to scratch and dig to gain ground in Mexican soil during their thirty-six-year struggle from political agreement on paper to steel reality—an unusually protracted length of time.

The country's first railroad concession in 1837 went to a Mexican—Francisco Arrillaga, a well-to-do merchant from Veracruz, who promised to carry the mails for free and to pay the government fifty thousand pesos a year for ten years in exchange for a thirty-year monopoly.[3] The line was to run from Veracruz to Mexico City. Yet Arrillaga failed to lay a single kilometer of track due to delays and lost the concession, which had stipulated the line be started within two years.

Mexican attitudes about the value of exclusively Mexican railroad investment ran hot and cold between 1837 and 1880 as the government both granted railroad concessions to foreigners and supported Mexican-owned lines. Antonio Lopez de Santa Anna (1822–1823, 1840–1844, 1853–1855), for instance, who had a "habitual willingness to alienate bits of Mexican territory or sovereignty," readily permitted both British and U.S. participation in railroad ventures, with concessions explicitly allowing participation by both countries.[4] But he also supported building Mexican lines with taxes from a variety of sources.[5] The interoceanic Tehuantepec Railroad, which has received extensive attention, also involved a mixture of Mexican, U.S., and British capital during its extremely long gestation.[6]

The French also wielded a strong influence. Their presence less than a decade earlier had marked Mexican elites with the influence of French philosophy, literature, and art. Emperor Ferdinand Maximilian's attitudes about railroads provide an interesting footnote that illustrates how a foreign-imposed government of Mexico could take a patriotic stand regarding railroads. In 1865, Maximilian's Ministry of Development emphasized the contributions that railroads would make to the country's future. Minister Luis Robles Pezuela saw railroads as a method for "implanting in the nacent [sic] empire a new era of progress." He stressed the idea that the state should play a leading role in forming a national railway network, avoiding the "excessively advantageous" terms given to the holders of the first concessions in France, England, and the United States.[7]

This French influence also specifically included Positivistic elements. Gabino Barreda, an education official under President Benito Juárez, had lived in Paris from 1847 to 1851 and had become a convert to the doctrine of Positivism. In 1867 he gave an oration in the town of Guanajuato espousing national education goals. In it he noted—

foreshadowing the Pax Porfiriano—"the key necessity of obtaining a uniformity of opinion among thinking people so as to insure Mexico from future conflict." Barreda concluded his speech with an appeal to patriotism that identified, by implication, Positivism with liberalism, and liberalism with Mexicanism. The slogan of the new world order would be "Libertad, Orden y Progreso."[8] The French had been largely responsible for promulgating Comte's Positivist philosophy. Mexican elites such as Barreda then coopted Positivist thought and defined it as Mexican for their purposes.

The desire to Mexicanize foreign elements also manifested itself in the sphere of railroads during the Restored Republic (1867–1876). Several of the country's railroad firms found clever ways to make their lines exclusively Mexican during this period. For instance, two of the companies constructing lines during the late years of the Restored Republic and the start of the Porfiriato (1876–1911) developed an ingenious method of getting at private financial resources in a country with very few formal financial institutions. The Mexico-Toluca-Cuautitlán and Mérida-Progreso companies instituted railroad lotteries, selling inexpensive lottery tickets to a large number of people in their regions, paying off the lottery winners, and then using the remaining monies for construction.

Despite these efforts, British influence remained strong. Finally completed on January 23, 1873, the Veracruz–Mexico City line became Mexico's first railroad, known as the Mexican Railway Company Limited. The Imperial Mexican Railway Company, a firm with English backing, completed the line.[9] Construction ultimately cost more than twelve times the original ten million pesos estimated by Arrillaga. President Sebastián Lerdo de Tejada presided over the opening ceremony and took a special interest in the line. It was, after all, the country's long-awaited first completed railroad and linked an important port city to the nation's capital.

When Porfirio Díaz took power in 1876, he excluded new British investors and generally discouraged U.S. railroad corporations from obtaining concessions. Díaz' government pushed insistently for railroad development without using foreign monies. He offered generous subsidies to Mexican companies, and his regime rapidly settled upon

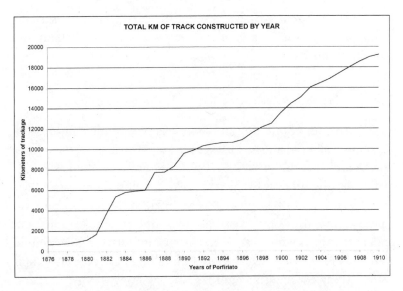

2.1 Total kilometers of track in Mexico constructed by year under Porfirio Díaz and Manuel González. (Courtesy of the author)

two primary strategies for promoting railroad construction. First, it invested public funds directly into small local railroad lines, entirely funding their construction. More importantly, the government adopted a policy of granting railroad concessions to state governments—an action that would have been nearly impossible before the Porfiriato, given the political fragmentation of the country.

By 1880, the Díaz government had given twenty states a total of twenty-eight concessions for a series of small lines. Only a minority of those concessions bore fruit, but eight of the twenty-eight concessions succeeded and grew (fig. 2.1). Díaz' early strategy represented his most consistent and well-thought-out approach to Mexican railroads. It also boosted Mexican pride, being widely and positively reported in the press. But as the Porfiriato continued, new Positivist elements arose within the government that encouraged foreign investment and looked increasingly to other countries to contribute to the country's progress. Díaz' own attitude about the value of foreign railroad investment also began to change. The end of Díaz' first term marked the termination of Mexico's brief experiment with Mexican-built and -owned railroads.

Changing Attitudes Towards the United States

North American ownership and control figured prominently in Mexican railroading after 1880. That year, in keeping with an earlier promise, Díaz did not run for office. He picked a successor, Manuel González, widely regarded as the least capable and most dishonest of Díaz' protégés and a weak rival should Díaz decide to run for another term in 1884.[10] President Gonazález began to court U.S. railroad capital and mining ventures with great vigor. During his four-year interregnum, railroad growth increased at a rapid clip. Within a decade after González' strong encouragement of U.S. capital, gringo-owned corporations operated many of the railroad lines in Mexico.

U.S. railroad companies began to build railroads in Mexico almost immediately after González took office. The two largest were the Mexican Central Railroad (MCR; Ferrocarril Central Mexicano)—for many years the westernmost railroad linking the border with Mexico City, terminating to the north at Ciudad Juárez)—and the NRM (with its northern terminus at Laredo, Texas, and its southern end in Mexico City). These great trunk lines provided both Mexico and the United States with cross-border rail passage. Both lines were chartered in 1880, within a week of each other. The MCR began after incorporation by a Massachusetts group and the NRM after incorporation by the Mexican National Construction Company of Colorado.[11] Both lines received generous concessions from González. With notable exceptions such as the SP de Mex, U.S. investors usually came to Mexico in the form of wealthy individuals, rather than taking the British approach of large corporations investing in and managing railroads in Latin America.

In the Porfirian decades after 1880, as U.S. railroad investment began to surge, observers in Mexico never had to look far to find opposing viewpoints about the U.S. railroad presence there. U.S. actions often provoked strong indignation in the Mexican press. Many writers expressed anti–U.S. sentiments, often without much precision but generally with a great deal of passion—implying strongly that U.S. companies were compromising the sovereignty of the nation by their strong presence in the country. For instance, the U.S. owners of the MCR sought in 1906 to require the use of English on their line but met with a storm of protest from various Mexican publications. "Ungrateful Yankees and the Means to Combat Them," read one news headline. The article continued: "This would be the most shameful humiliation that the United States of North America could cause to Mexico, even more than other instances we sadly recall; but today the *norteamericanos* have shown that they shame themselves."[12]

By 1908 the government had followed the lead of the press and began to support the need for Spanish-only rules. As Secretary of Finance José Ives Limantour remarked in 1908, the year that the NRM was organized: "Now that the railroads have been nationalized, it is the most natural thing that all of the details of service are conducted in Spanish, because the language is the most sensible manifestation of nationality of a people."[13]

Limantour played a large and well-known role in the anti–U.S. sentiment expressed in government circles during the Porfiriato. But despite expressing pro-Mexican sentiments like the one above, he and his group of científicos continued to hold conflicting attitudes about the value of U.S.–owned railroads. They would issue patriotic statements while at the same time pointing to the nationbuilding role played by the largely foreign railroads. And their views included racist and classist attitudes about the role and value of the railroad. They encouraged English-only rules for the operation of the railroad which excluded most Mexican laborers and considered the better-educated and foreign-born as superior. These views often blurred indistinguishably with those of their neighbors to the north.[14]

The Científicos

The científicos, a complex group of Positivist-, progress-, and technology-oriented men, occupied positions at various levels within the structure of Díaz' government. A small, informal cadre of intellectuals, they were established by Manuel Romero Rubio, Díaz' secretary of the interior. This group, which included governors and prominent members of the federal administration, openly recognized Limantour as its leader. As the person overseeing Mexico's rapidly growing transportation network, the brilliant but erratic Limantour wielded especially strong influence over científico attitudes about the Mexican and foreign railroads operating throughout the country. His high position in Díaz' cabinet also meant that he lent prestige and power to the científicos, who would have had far less influence without him.[15]

A number of factions wrestled for ideological supremacy within the government, although most of these struggles were clandestine due to Díaz' power. Díaz himself covertly encouraged General Bernardo Reyes, the head of the War Department, to oppose the científicos when he felt that they had consolidated more informal power than he was comfortable with.[16] Reyes, who had considerable ambivalence about Díaz' leadership, broke with the president in 1885 in order to join forces with the caudillos in northern Mexico. Reyes manifested an influential form of regionalism because of his powerful personality and prominence in both Sonoran and national affairs, and these regionally driven impulses often ran counter to Mexico City's desires.[17]

Díaz' científicos were proud of Mexican railroads and of the qualities they implied—including punctuality, technical advancement, and even the ways that trains appeared to modify space and time itself. As one writer on nineteenth-century railroads has noted: "The railroad did not appear embedded in the space of the landscape the way coach and highway are, but seemed to strike its way through it."[18] To the científicos, the train was progress. And as it had also appeared to nineteenth-century Brazilian Positivists, the railroad journey was a form of pugilism, a blur of unassailable movement and strength. They considered progress not just as a vague concept, but as physical forward momentum—literally, nothing could stand its ground against a two-hundred-ton locomotive roaring down the track.

But ironically, despite Mexican pride in the country's lines and the "progressive" attributes accompanying the railroad, the científicos calling for a modern vision of Mexico derived their inspiration from outside the country. In fact, they had more in common with the U.S.

railroad administrators doing business in Mexico, and with most U.S. businessmen, politicians, and journalists, than might be assumed in light of the historical enmity and the tensions that existed almost constantly between the two countries. Groups in both nations often made racist pronouncements about portions of Mexico's populations, especially about the more indigenous population of the northwest.

Mexico's class and race hierarchy was, and remains, highly fluid. Perceptions of a person's racial status could change with their social status, and in fact, citizens could actually purchase a "certificate of whiteness"—a *carnet de blanco*—that gave them a new social status based on their ability to pay for the certificate. Race was thus tied much more closely to class than to phenotype, as it is in the United States.

And so it was for the científicos. To them, racism was not as much a distinction between skin colors as it was a judgment based on traditional methods of work, transportation, and subsistence versus more modern conceptions of technology. Anyone moving "slowly"—usually the native population, in their eyes—was "backwards" and "slumbering." As Pablo Macedo, a científico who was president of the Federal Congress and director of two banks and the Pan-American Railway, remarked exultantly in 1902: "At the strident whistle of the locomotive crossing many parts of its territory, the nation has awakened from its long sleep."[19] The echo of Macedo's sentiments could often be heard in U.S. circles in the same language; as a *Washington Post* headline about Sonoran development noted in 1906, "Yankees Arousing Old Senora [*sic*] From Long Period of Slumber."[20]

Limantour himself bore the racist standard for the científicos. As he told the National Science Conference in 1901, "the weak, the unprepared, those who lack the tools in order to emerge victorious against evolution, must perish and leave the struggle to the more powerful."[21] It was a perverted social application of Darwin's theory of natural selection—echoed and perhaps influenced by U.S. social Darwinist attitudes—and a convenient "scientific" justification for the ruthless exercise of power.

By the start of the twentieth century, both Mexican- and foreign-owned railroads played a fundamental role in the life of the country.

They carried nearly eight million metric tons of goods each year. Passengers logged nearly a billion kilometers of travel annually over their lines, and the country's railroads paid 145 million pesos into the Treasury.[22]

But foreign involvement in the lines made it clear to Porfirian leaders that a defining element was missing: regulations and laws governing extranational involvement in Mexican railroads. No consistent regulations governed their operations, and no authoritative group oversaw the country's lines, either foreign- or Mexican-owned. Awareness slowly grew in government circles: the country's railroad system required fundamental changes if Mexican railroads were to become more efficient. These concerns led directly to the first pieces of government legislation designed to regulate Mexican railroads.

Government Regulation of Mexican Railroads, 1877–1909

The critical railroad law enacted in 1899 and the formation of the NRM in 1908 had an evolutionary base beginning in 1876. When Díaz first took office he informally placed railroad affairs under the Department of Public Welfare (Departamento de Fomento), which oversaw all public works in Mexico. In 1877, Díaz then created the office of Inspector of Railroads within the department. This office was responsible in theory for creating all rules and regulations to govern the operations and services of railroads within Mexico. But, like the first Argentine railroad legislation in 1872, Mexico's initial attempt at government control of the lines did not adequately manage the country's growing number of concessions for new lines.

Reacting to slowly but steadily increasing foreign investment in mining, González introduced a liberal mining code in 1884 that softened the traditional Spanish mining law. The new law retained requirements for periodic government inspection but relinquished government ownership of nonmetallic deposits such as oil. The law, designed to accelerate the flow of foreign capital into the mining industry, surpassed government expectations. In a single year, the González government registered over two thousand titles to new mines.[23] Petroleum mines made up a considerable portion of these new extractive efforts, and the country's prominence as a world oil supplier soared. And as mining boomed, railroads grew even more quickly. González' administration granted "railroad concessions with subsidy to all who asked for them, without measure or prudence . . . without order or method."[24]

Rigorous growth did not mean equally rigorous control, and improved Mexican management of the country's railroads became increasingly urgent. A new Department of Communications and Public Works (SCOP; Secretaría de Comunicaciones y Obras Públicas) was created for this purpose on May 13, 1891—one of seven ministries created by Díaz as part of the new secretary of finance (secretaría de hacienda). The SCOP had jurisdiction over telegraph and telephone service, the mails, water transportation, highways, and other forms of transportation and communication, including the railroads.

Limantour played a central role in Mexico's railroad regulation. He entered office as secretary of finance in 1892, overseeing SCOP, and soon became the dominant member of the Díaz government, initiating many of its policies. Under his watchful eye, a host of bureaucrats wrote and published guidelines for operation and management, and legislation slowly grew in detail and quantity.[25] It took some time for the SCOP under Limantour to gain prestige and recognition as a legitimate governing body, and it thus took several years for laws to have any practical effect.

No good precedents existed in nineteenth-century Latin America for providing mechanisms to control railroads. By 1890, neither Argentina nor Brazil had yet established effective models for regulating their rapidly growing rail networks. Argentina's General Railway Law 2873 remained inadequate, and Brazilian railroad growth up to the end of the Brazilian Empire had consisted of very little regulation in the face of laissez-faire liberalism and the abundant profits of coffee. Existing scraps of legislation, both outside and inside of Mexico, remained regional, piecemeal, and sometimes contradictory.

Meanwhile, Díaz and his cabinet recognized the growing importance of a line leading along the west coast towards Mexico City. Díaz realized that a transportation link to the north could increase his military and political control of this area. Writing in 1896 to a potential investor who wanted to run a line southward along the coast from Topolobampo, through the same territory the SP de Mex would cross a decade later, Díaz responded: "I hasten to tell you that should anybody submit serious propositions, in an official manner, for the organization of a Company having the means to build that very important road, the Department will take said proposition into consideration, and will, no doubt, give it a resolution in the most favorable manner according to law, and to suit public requirements."[26]

But railroad construction and growth in "the most favorable manner according to law" and even the "public requirements" noted by Díaz were vague concepts that did not translate well into specific actions. The question of how—and how much—to control the nation's railroads continued to loom large throughout the Porfiriato. Although much discussion had taken place about creating a government organization to oversee and manage all railroads in the country, many in Díaz' cabinet feared that such centralization would upset U.S. companies and stimulate competing foreign railroad concerns (such as the two rival U.S. firms controlling the country's large trunk lines, the MCR and the NRM) to stop competing and join forces to resist any kind of regulatory body Mexico might create.

Díaz and Limantour also at first disagreed sharply on the role foreign companies should be allowed to play. Díaz wanted to promote economic growth and, after 1880, increasingly supported U.S. railroad concerns interested in operating in Mexico. In doing so, he showed a willingness to let less stable and more speculative U.S. railroad ventures into the country. In 1898, Limantour presented Díaz with a report that pointed out the necessity of modifying the government's practice of granting heavy concessions and subsidies to such a wide range of foreign companies. Narrowing the types of concessions granted would help conserve the nation's financial strength, the secretary argued.

The 1899 Railroad Law

Díaz found Limantour's argument compelling. The proposed new law, the 1899 Railroad Law, was a major piece of legislation overseen by Limantour. The Mexican Congress approved the law unanimously with the backing of both men, and the Act became law on May 13, 1899. The exceptionally heavy U.S. railroad presence in Mexico— railroad investments would reach $644.3 million U.S. by 1910 and would consist of 61.7 percent of all U.S. investment in the country— demanded correspondingly detailed and strong legislation.[27] The voluminous act consisted of 187 articles divided into fourteen chapters containing detailed provisions governing classification of railroads; concessions; forfeiture of concessions; nationality and legal status; construction; operation; rights reserved to the nation; jurisdiction over the lines; and more. New concessions no longer required Congressional approval, but the law specified stricter conditions for issuance of new concessions and set priorities for the granting of government subsidies.[28]

The científicos had a longstanding desire for national unity but had lacked a specific approach to foster it. The 1899 law provided them with a plan to breathe life into that desire. They thus had high hopes for the law. "This document," noted Deputy Macedo six years after its passage, "marks the precise moment in our railroad history in which we paused to consider the ground covered, the methods which we had employed, and above all what was left to be done and how to do it within the scope of a well defined national plan."[29] The new law offered the hope for many científicos that order in the form of railroad legislation, and progress in the form of the railroad itself, would finally come together to fully epitomize Positivist thought.

The legislation stipulated that railroad construction would be favored along eight general routes—what the law called "routes of prime importance"; limitation on the construction of parallel lines (to prevent competition for certain routes and thus allow both the government and the foreign owners to enjoy the benefits of monopoly); and a whole host of other items that spelled out and standardized aspects of railroad operations for the first time. The law also covered details not included in its later Argentine counterpart, the Mitre Law of 1907, such as specific guidelines for compensation of nationalized lines (very equitable in Mexico's case: a payment equal to the par value of the company's stock plus 10 percent).

But unlike their government counterparts in Argentina, Porfirian officials did not move strongly and consistently to enforce the well-drafted law. For instance, only three of the eight primary routes suggested by the law reached completion by the end of Díaz' reign. Mexico remained ambivalent about the role of U.S. railroad capital between 1900 and 1909 because deep internal divisions over the degree of appropriate railroad control existed among Díaz, Limantour, and various railroad functionaries within the government.

In the process of drafting railroad law, Mexico also closely watched North American examples of regulation. In the United States, a similar attempt at nationwide control had been tried in the form of the Interstate Commerce Act (ICA) of 1887. But it was clear to Mexico that the U.S. government's early efforts at railroad regulation were almost laughable in their ineffectiveness. For instance, the ICA stipulated that all fees for interstate rail transportation be "reasonable and just" but failed to furnish a standard or method to determine these criteria. The Interstate Commerce Commission (ICC), a five-person agency, was supposed to administer the act, although the commissioners did not have enforcement powers. Many in U.S. government and business loved the ICC, because the commission satisfied the political exigencies of having a supposed governing body yet did not make business suffer at all.[30]

The ICA strove for a high regulatory ideal, even if it was weakly implemented. Ironically, Mexico emulated this pattern closely: well-drafted but poorly realized legislation. The same problem plagued both countries. Their respective governments feared that powerful corporations would exercise inordinate control over the country's economy, but no one wanted to offend the railroads because their lines benefited many sectors of the population, especially the rule-making elite. In some ways, the same scenario also applied in Brazil, where exceptionally strong reliance on coffee meant that government officials were not eager to risk driving out railroad companies in the coffee infrastructure.

Despite these anxieties, the concept of progress still remained constantly on the lips and pens of the científico elite in Mexico City up to the very end of Díaz' rule. Espousing the virtues of progress provided one way to avoid coping with the dichotomy of foreign involvement versus self-reliance. And northern Mexico, despite being far from the capital, was populated with Positivists as well.

In fact, Reyes, whom Díaz had asked to oppose the científicos before the two men split, represented a northern form of Positivism that maintained the notion of scientific progress from the last days of the Porfiriato well into the revolution. "Spirit, faith and energy! Tomorrow corresponds completely with progress, and progress is democracy," Reyes noted exuberantly in a 1909 letter to his neighbor, future Sonoran governor José Maria Maytorena.[31] Positivist thought lived on passionately in northern Mexico—a location it has rarely been described as inhabiting. Although científicos usually identified themselves as Positivists, not all Positivists considered themselves to be científicos. As Maytorena noted to Reyes's son Rodolfo in 1909, "The politics of the científicos never will be popular, because they will never truly be able to interest the masses, which, as you well know, allow themselves to be guided more by passion than by reason, which will always be cold and analytical."[32]

In Mexico City, the científicos continued to struggle with issues related to administration of the railroad. By 1903, Reyes's alter ego, Limantour, had decided to take more active steps to Mexicanize railroads without alienating foreign owners. He initiated a program whereby the government would buy railroad stock from various foreign and Mexican concerns in order to gain a controlling interest in those lines. This way, he reasoned, the government could have a significant say in the operations of the railroad without having to actually run or staff the lines. The holdings would then be part of an umbrella organization known as the National Railways of Mexico, or NRM (Ferrocarriles Nacionales de México). This was a brilliant maneuver by Limantour, because Mexico could thus gain control of many lines, yet avoid alienating lucrative U.S. investors by providing profits for U.S. railroad companies through purchase of their stock. It also provided a new form of regulatory control.

Limantour himself realized that geographically the country's lines did not fully serve Mexican needs. In 1908, he declared to the Mexican Congress that "the location of the lines leaves much to be desired, in the conflict between the desires of the capital building the lines and the interests of the diverse regions through which the railroads pass. Each day we resent more and more the inconveniences that accrue from this building taking place without having a general plan."[33] The time was ripe for a national railroad organization with a strong and definable structure—again, a first in Latin American railroading. While Argentina's Mitre Law of 1907 provided detailed and effective legislation to allow effective government control, the proposed Mexican solution would give Mexico the promise, at least, of an umbrella organization with a managing board, stock ownership, and other methods that would allow the government a means to regulate and manage Mexican railroads.

The NRM, 1908–1910

The NRM, also known colloquially as the NdeM, was incorporated on March 28, 1908. The government decree leading to incorporation stated that its capital would consist of 460 million pesos. The company issued an initial offering of 75 million pesos of common stock—750,000 shares at 100 pesos each, with 99 percent of the stock going into public hands.[34] The organization got off to a good start. By the end of 1910, the new corporation had become the majority shareholder in five standard lines and five narrow-gauge lines, virtually all of which had been built by some combination of foreign capital. Of these ten lines, only the narrow-gauge Hidalgo and Northeastern Railroad had been built solely with Mexican capital. The ten lines totaled 12,566 kilometers of trackage; with yards and sidings the amount came to 13,595 kilometers by the end of the Porfiriato.[35]

Enthusiasm for this form of government control of the railroad ran high. The law creating the NRM provided excellent direction and explicit guidance.[36] Some saw the new organization as a critical element of Mexican independence and national pride. Noted Jaime Gurza, a top Porfirian railroad administrator, "Every effort, which like the nationalization of our railroads gives us more independence and more influence in our internal affairs and relations, must be eminently patriotic."[37]

But despite such widely published expressions of nationalist sentiment, Limantour still did not exorcise the demon of foreign interests through formation of the NRM, an organization that has received remarkably little study. One of the strangest and most contradictory aspects of the NRM was the makeup of its board of directors. The congressional decree that created the NRM stated specifically that the company would be "governed in the City of Mexico by a Board of twenty-one directors, of whom nine may reside abroad and may constitute a local board which may meet in New York."[38] This setup was a concession to the fact that many of the railroads pulled together under the aegis of the NRM were funded by foreign (particularly U.S.) money, but it seems an incredible contradiction that an organization created expressly to nationalize Mexican railroads could be significantly controlled by non-Mexicans, as it soon was.

Government officials set up this arrangement so that the New York board could legally represent the lines' creditors, many of which were U.S.–based financial institutions, and could dispose of the company's property at will if it failed to meet its obligations. However, in practice, it meant that the organization actually had two Boards of Directors, because the nine members of the board in New York had powers equal to the other twenty-two members in Mexico City. A constant tension would exist in the years to come between the U.S. members of the board and their Mexican counterparts. Furthermore, the ideological inconsistency of Mexican railroad control through the mechanism of a foreign governing body steadily eroded attitudes about the Mexicanness of the national lines until Cárdenas (1934–1940) changed the structure of the organization.

In administering the NRM, Limantour had other goals besides gaining governmental control of the growing foreign-owned and -run railroad lines. He expressed the belief that via railroad consolidation a number of inefficiencies could be eliminated or reduced. For instance, lines in Mexico before the NRM were a thicket of redundant or unnecessary trackage, often created for short-term gain or to serve specific markets, with no regard for other lines in the vicinity. Through a conglomerate of lines, Limantour reasoned, traffic could be carried over the best and shortest routes, and other economies of operation could be effected.

But just as Mexico began to realize increased efficiencies of operation and administration of the nation's rail service, the Mexican Revolution flared to life. The NRM's operations during the conflict illustrate the vitality and robustness of Mexican railroad operations through 1915, despite increasing turmoil in the country.

The NRM during the Mexican Revolution

The annual reports of the NRM during the first five years of the Mexican Revolution paint a detailed and surprising picture of the organization's financial gains. The reports show that the NRM turned significant profits well into 1914 despite rapid increases in the national debt and despite the fact that the federal government consistently allocated only 10 to 15 percent of its annual budget to communications and public works.[39] Upon the eve of the revolution, ten different railroads did business over the nearly nine million kilometers of track under NRM control, and the company made more than twenty million pesos profit out of their gross earnings of fifty-two million pesos.[40] The new organization had made a terrific start.

The first rumblings of change in Mexico in late 1910 and early 1911 apparently had little effect on NRM operations. The company gobbled up the stock of the Veracruz-Isthmus Railway (known in later years as the Isthmus Railway) and the Pan American Railroad Company. These two lines provided critical transportation links in southern Mexico. The NRM made even more money in 1911, netting 23.6 million pesos from their gross income of 62 million pesos. It also continued to make improvements along the various lines, sinking artisan wells, planting trees, and making various improvements to tracks and structures.

The NRM's fourth annual report, for the year ended June 1, 1912, then reveals startling information. Despite the political unraveling of increasingly larger segments of the country in 1912, and more frequent and serious confrontations between federal troops and such diverse groups as Zapatista guerrillas to the south and Pascual Orozco's and Pancho Villa's uprisings to the north in Chihuahua, the NRM continued to grow in size and reap large profits. Of a gross income of 61.4 million pesos, the company netted 21.9 million pesos. The number of

NRM employees also increased, to 31,179. Only 639 workers, or 2.05 percent, were foreigners—the result of their removal by Francisco Madero, one of the key instigators of the Mexican Revolution, after a series of strikes.

Although no new lines were acquired that year, the annual report summarized the extraordinary success of Mexican railroads during increasingly troubled times: "Taking into consideration . . . the unsettled political conditions which have obtained throughout the Republic during the last five months of the fiscal year, the results can only be considered as remarkable and evidencing the wonderful vitality of the country."[41]

While "vitality" may not have been the most accurate descriptor that officials could have selected to illustrate Mexico's overall condition, the detailed figures in the report tell a story of solid railroad growth and increased freight and passenger traffic for 1912, and that growth was indeed noteworthy given the turmoil of Mexico that year. Even more surprising, the next year of 1913 was equally profitable, netting 21.3 million pesos on a gross of 57.3 million pesos. Despite these gains, the number of employees dropped by nearly 20 percent, to 25,852. The railroad was doing well even with significantly less manpower.

Nineteen fourteen was the first difficult year of NRM operations, although still a profitable one, albeit marginally. The NRM grossed twenty-one million pesos and netted only a million pesos profit—a far cry from the years between 1908 and 1913 but a profit nonetheless. The company's various lines also logged a total of 86 million kilometers of freight and passenger traffic. The rail network rolled along well despite the highly publicized stories of mass railroad destruction in the Mexican press that year.

When U.S. forces occupied Veracruz in late April of 1914, President Victoriano Huerta ordered all U.S. employees of the NRM out of the country. One can almost hear the quiver of emotion in the voice of C. R. Hudson, NRM vice president, who noted that "the very best was done that could be done under the circumstances. It is doubtful if a set of operating officers were ever called upon to face such extraordinary conditions in the operation of a railway, as were your officers in the year under review."[42]

Venustiano Carranza's Constitucionalistas finally achieved a very rough-edged consolidation of power by year's end. On November 18, 1914, Venustiano Carranza coopted most of the NRM under the auspices of what he called the National Constitutional Railroads (NCR; Ferrocarriles Constitucionalistas de México). Because Carranza could not surgically remove the firm's U.S. board members, nor shift its business operations to a totally Mexican form, he simply ignored the NRM's existing organizational structure and claimed the system as his own. He kicked out all the employees in the NRM headquarters in Mexico City and took their personal possessions as well as the furniture out of the building, taking or destroying company archives, the safe containing funds and receipts, and physically or administratively dismantling other important parts of the NRM's operations.[43]

NRM officials still considered theirs the most important railroad institution in Mexico. But Carranza felt differently. Because of the Carrancista cooption of many thousands of kilometers of line, and no corresponding publication of operating figures for those coopted lines, business statistics for the NRM between 1915 and 1920 are naturally inaccurate as a reflection of the system's total operations. However, the NRM reported in June 1915 that they had grossed just 1.8 million pesos and had a net loss of 28.9 million pesos, approximately the amount they owed to their various creditors each year. Debts remained stable, but income plummeted.

The NCR, 1914–1920

"Railroad lines constitute a circulatory system of the national organism," remarked Alberto J. Pani, the nearly omnipotent director of railroads under Carranza.[44] Pani and Carranza both considered railroad operations a very high priority during the second half of the military phase of the revolution. Although relatively little material has come to light detailing Carranza's operations of the lines between 1915 and 1920, he did coopt the NRM lines completely and kept them running both nationally and internationally. In contrast to John H. McNeely's incorrect statement that "while the Carranza government was in power . . . movement of cars from the United States into

Mexico was not reestablished until January 1, 1921,"[45] U.S. consular reports show that traffic crossed quite fluidly to and from the United States throughout Carranza's time in office. While Carranza sharply raised rates for the shipment of ore to and from mines, most of which were U.S.–owned or –operated properties, to the exasperation of the U.S. State Department, he in fact encouraged cross-border transportation for the income generated by the higher tariffs charged to U.S. companies as they entered Mexico.[46]

The NRM's operations between 1910 and 1915 offer a useful look at some of the revolution's workings. The railroad's ability to operate relatively undisturbed through 1913 was probably due to reluctance on the part of various revolutionary factions to destroy railroads they considered strategically important or symbolic. Until 1913, these factions preferred to operate the lines for military advantage as carriers of troops and essential supplies. But beginning in 1914, *revolucionarios* apparently favored destruction of the lines in an attempt to stop others from using them. Railroad destruction did not focus disproportionately on any one region between 1914 and 1915, but took place throughout the country. This change in approach reflected the increasing desperation and frustration of not just some but virtually all of the factions jockeying for position.

No one could keep the upper hand for long. An anarchical malaise settled over Mexico in 1914, and it reflected the sense of frustration and hopelessness felt by large portions of the population. Destruction was widespread. It has been estimated that by 1915 as many as half of all the standard-gauge boxcars in Mexico had been destroyed, while hundreds of the locomotives in the country had met the same fate.[47]

But the Carrancista machine continued doggedly, keeping as many lines running as possible. The worst years for the NCR were 1915 and 1916. The Carrancista machine "officially" ran the national railway system from November 18, 1914 to September 1, 1916 and then again from April 3, 1917 until June 9, 1920—a total of about fifty-nine months, or half the revolutionary period from 1910 to 1920.

In contrast to the high percentage of non-Mexican administrators on the NRM's board of directors between 1909 and 1914, Carranza kept Mexican railroad operations strictly in Mexican hands. The main

concern of Carranza's chief railroad officer, Pani, was supplying Mexico City with adequate food and goods. Pani pointed to three factors
that made moving supplies into Mexico City difficult: first, a great
scarcity of rolling stock; second, "intervention from extraneous authorities"; and third, "the lack of morality of certain military elements
as well as some railroad employees."[48]

Pani worked hard to overcome these obstacles, maintaining an
ironclad rule over the NCR railroad system. He continually affirmed
the sovereignty of Mexico's railroads, and his attitudes provided a
counterpoint to the mixed nationality of the board members who had
governed the NRM. In September 1915, Carranza signed a decree
conferring absolute regulatory power to Director General Pani—an
authority the thirty-eight-year-old former engineer reinforced in
November with a memorandum affirming his responsibilities and his
loyalties: "Once and for all, The Director General of the NCR declares
that in fulfillment of his official duties he recognizes neither parentage
nor relationships nor friendships, neither can he protect private interests when they are incompatible with the general interest, neither can
he authorize infractions which may weaken discipline . . ."[49]

Carranza and Pani both treated Mexico's internal railroad operations carefully and responsibly. Carranza forced soldiers who had
joined the army and then gone to work for the railroads to renounce
their military status, noting the possible conflict of interest. He and
Pani also carefully drafted plan after plan to keep freight traffic flowing into and out of Mexico City, in order to prevent the country's
freight circulation from becoming "anemic."[50]

Despite this care, the NRM lost money rapidly during the 1915–
1920 period, continuing the downward slide started by revolutionary
upheaval in 1914. What came to be known as "the railroad problem"
received substantial ink from Mexican writers. Although many wrote
about the system's poor financial state and suggested a variety of ways
to resuscitate the lines, a larger issue received the most attention: How
could Mexican railroads best serve the country's own needs, rather
than simply providing income to foreign investors?[51]

The solutions suggested were rarely one-dimensional or even technical, and often verged on being poetic in nature. This was because

railroads had rooted themselves so deeply into the Mexican landscape that some writers saw the railroad as a force of nature. Others viewed the railroad more specifically as a force of nature that had simply been given the wrong stimuli. For instance, Fernando González Roa, a railroad engineer, noted that "the development of the railroads, as experienced under General Díaz, went against the natural order of things." Roa also expressed his sense of the railroad as a vital component of nationbuilding: "Examining our past experience, the nation must get on the path to development of its railroads until the network is completed and it is able to satisfy the needs of the nation."[52] In his view, physical completion of the lines would lead to psychic as well as financial security for the country and a strengthened sense of *patria*.

As the end of his rule approached and Mexico prepared for legal elections, Carranza transferred the NRM back to its owners in early 1920, without incident or bloodshed. Despite the ravages of the revolution, most of the railroad's infrastructure remained intact. But within weeks of President Alvaro Obregón's taking office in December 1920, foreign countries began to press the government insistently to make reparations for damages suffered during the revolution. In June 1922, Obregón invited the U.S.–based International Committee on Bankers (ICB) to Mexico to discuss a loan. Adolfo de la Huerta, secretary of finance, and Thomas W. Lamont, president of the ICB, agreed to a series of very large loans from the United States to Mexico. Known as the Bucareli Agreements, these loans fixed the country's railroad debt at nearly a quarter-billion dollars—nearly half of Mexico's total indebtedness to the United States. The loan papers were signed, and the amount owed was included as part of the general public indebtedness of Mexico.[53]

Because of this new financial obligation to its northern neighbor, driven by Obregón's desire for U.S. recognition, Mexico was again not free to maintain its own railroad destiny—this time, not merely because of anxieties about how U.S. corporations might react to any tighter regulation and more thorough nationalization of the lines, but because the country was financially indebted to a consortium of U.S. and European bankers for an enormous sum of money. This set of frustrations would strongly influence Mexican relations with the SP de Mex.

As railroads grew during the Porfiriato, Mexican politicians expressed their attitudes about the contributions the country's lines made to national unity and progress. ". . . with the railroads were we born into the life of civilization," proclaimed científico Macedo at the turn of the century.[54] Limantour urged Díaz to consider authorizing only those lines that would best serve the country as a whole.[55] Federal Deputy Macedo, who served as Limantour's closest collaborator on the organization of the national lines, compared the country's railroads to a single corpus: "[The country's railroads are] breaking the bonds of its ligaments, extending its own arteries where previously there had only circulated a little discolored blood, and with this, life has begun to be felt."[56] Many prominent government and labor officials considered the nation's railroads to be a single unit, or desired them to serve as such, and they referred to the network as a whole rather than a compilation of regional elements or advantages in their pronouncements.

Porfirian observers and railroad administrators considered "Positivism-as-conquest" and the role of the railroad as a penetrator of the Mexican landscape to be desirable. Furthermore, their neighbors to the north also shared some of these views. The fact that much of the press and leading politicians in both countries saw the railroad as a conqueror and penetrator thus contributed to the lack of a clear and distinct Mexican attitude about the railroad. Observers in both countries held notions of Mexico as a backwards and slumbering land that the railroad was capable of stirring to life.

To many in the Mexican government, especially the científicos, the railroads' unifying, conquering role came first, and the significance of their origins came second. As in southeastern Brazil, the profitability railroads brought to Mexico outweighed any perceived or real erosion of sovereignty. However, late in the Porfiriato increased unease about the heavy role played by U.S. capital led to regulatory efforts designed to bring a modicum of control to Mexican railroading. Limantour drove much of this change in attitude, championing the 1899 Railroad Law as well as creation of the NRM in 1908.

Unfortunately, the outbreak of revolution interrupted what might have been a smooth and steady transition from U.S. to Mexican control of the country's lines, comparable to Argentina's experience after 1907. Instead, the conflict exacerbated Mexican distrust of U.S. activities in general, stemming from such encroachments as the bombing, invasion, and occupation of Veracruz, Pershing's Punitive Expedition, and other attempted or successful dalliances in Mexican affairs. One outgrowth of the revolution that affected the nation generally, but also applies specifically to the presence of foreign railroads, was an increased awareness of the dangers of having a much more powerful border neighbor. As a result of the conflict, Mexico's relationship with the United States went from that of financial partner to that of antagonist and, with the Bucareli Agreements, to the role of supplicant and dependent.

The end of the revolution and Obregón's ascension to power did not automatically lead to firmer Mexican control over the country's railroads, despite increased awareness of the dangers inherent in having close commercial ties to the United States. Although Mexico realized the growing need for Mexican sovereignty, and although Mexico's railroads provided a symbol of self-sufficiency, progress, and growth, numerous contradictions existed. The government owned majority shares in most Mexican railroads but a foreign board of directors still oversaw them. The country's lines had provided revolutionary war heroes with a vehicle for victory but the damages done to a number of U.S. railroads by military forces had contributed to the country's indebtedness to U.S. and European bankers. Given these circumstances and tensions, it is clear why Mexico's two important pieces of railway legislation—the 1899 Railroad Law and the 1908 creation of the NRM—did not provide the government with precise and fully realized control of Mexican railroads.

To add more complexity to Mexico's web of railroad management, one large and active line—the SP de Mex—fell outside the jurisdiction of the NRM. Because of its vital strategic importance, control and regulation of the line was very important to the government. Several factors made the dance between the government and the railroad a very delicate one.

Mexico considered completion and operation of the line to be a high commercial and military priority. However, the line's U.S. ownership was problematic to the government for a number of reasons. The NRM could not control the SP de Mex in the same ways it managed railroads under its own umbrella because the U.S.–owned railroad had no public stock offering. And as the only railroad entering the country west of Ciudad Juárez, the SP de Mex had an undesirable ability to control the flow of goods in and out of northwestern Mexico. Finally, the railroad had the potential to control military and commercial access to most of the Pacific Ocean because of its coast-hugging location—a particularly sensitive issue to Mexico in light of the ease with which U.S. forces had penetrated the country in search of Villa.

What decisions would the Mexican government make to maximize the strategic, commercial, and political value of the SP de Mex, while minimizing the risks to Mexican sovereignty inherent in a line starting north of the border and run by a large, powerful U.S. company? The examination and analysis of Mexican treatment of the line constitutes the rest of this study.

CHAPTER 3

The Revolution, Reparations, and the Railroad (1909–1923)

The northwest coast of Mexico—that broad band of land along the Pacific Ocean consisting of the states of Sonora, Sinaloa, Nayarit, and Jalisco—had no transportation link by railroad to the rest of the country until 1927, despite the great importance government and civic leaders had placed on the region since nationhood. Part of this separation from the rest of Mexico stemmed from the presence of the Sierra Madre Occidental, a broadly sloping range of mountains running southward from eastern Sonora down to Guadalajara. Geographers term this region the Northwest Pacific Coastlands, and the coastal plain contained by the mountains consists of a mass of land 1,100 kilometers long and averaging 50 kilometers wide. Although the mountains hampered national commerce and communications, relative isolation helped to give the region its own identity.

Sonora—flat, hot, and dry in most areas of the state—averages a scant twenty centimeters of rainfall per year. Mines in such towns as Cananea, Tonichi, and Alamos, many worked since colonial rule, produced great quantities of copper, gold, and silver, and dot the countryside. But the landscape and the climate change to the south in Sinaloa. Long and club-shaped, with 550 kilometers of coastline, the state of Sinaloa has higher rainfall and more hospitable soil than Sonora. A strip of rich land stretches for hundreds of kilometers down the full length of the state and continues well into Nayarit. Sugar has grown successfully here for hundreds of years, and sugar plantations—some of the largest in Mexico—stretch for hundreds of

3.1 Leased SP Consolidation train, on *mixto* No. 1, roaring up the 3 percent grade near Hidalgo, Sonora, a dozen kilometers north of Nacozari, ca. 1958. (Courtesy of Donald Duke, Golden West Books, San Marino, California)

kilometers in the region's rich black soil; tomatoes and winter vegetables have also thrived and been grown in vast quantities.

The long western coast plain finally ends just after crossing the Santiago River in the state of Nayarit and becomes more fertile, with rainfall increasing to seventy-five centimeters annually, the majority of it falling during the summer. The southern end of the coast plain then encounters the central table of Mexico: a geographic upheaval that created a ragged series of gorges and ravines in the barrancas region. South of the barrancas, the altitude increases to an elevation of nine hundred meters, the temperature cools, and the terrain becomes broad and rolling. These geographic features provided a series of construction challenges to the railroad and offered varied scenery for travelers aboard the Southern Pacific of Mexico (SP de Mex; Ferrocarril Sud-Pacífico de México) (fig. 3.1).

The cultural geography of the Sonoran region in particular also played an important role in the railroad's fortunes. Populated by Yaqui Indians, Chinese immigrants, and Mormon workers, Sonora became an especially difficult flashpoint for difficulties in the railroad's relationship with local ethnic groups as well as with the federal government. Furthermore, the SP de México's own company town in Empalme created discrepancies in treatment and status, which caused a different brand of resentment, as we shall see.

No other railroad in Mexico penetrated the Sierra Madre Occidental during the life of the SP de Mex, although the government finally completed the Chihuahua-Pacífico line from Chihuahua into the port city of Topolobampo in 1961, after a lengthy struggle across the mountains at a cost of 104 million pesos.[1] Until 1961, the line nearest to the west coast region was the Mexican Central Railroad (MCR; Ferrocarril Central Mexicano), terminating to the north in Ciudad Juárez. Three different lines have operated in or near Mexico's west coast: the Cananea, Río Yaquí y Pacífico, a short line of several hundred kilometers running from Arizona to the copper mines at Cananea for about twenty years; the Kansas City, Mexico & Orient, a line running from Topolobampo towards the Sierra Madre Occidental but never completed across the mountains as intended; and the SP de Mex. Only one, the SP de Mex—a section of which was known as the Sonora Railway from its incorporation in 1879 until the Southern Pacific Company (SP) took over operations in 1898—ever connected with Mexico City, providing a vital strategic and commercial link by rail along the west coast from the capital to northern Sonora.

The Sonora Railway Company Limited was incorporated on April 29, 1879. Its first owners—the U.S.–based Atcheson, Topeka & Santa Fe railroad company (AT&SF)—planned for the line to run from Nogales on the Mexico–U.S. border down to the small port town of Guaymas, 422 kilometers to the southwest. It was the first U.S. railroad ever to incorporate in Mexico. President Porfirio Díaz, just beginning to experiment in a limited fashion with U.S. railroad investment, provided the Sonora Railway with a ninety-nine-year lease and a subsidy of nine thousand pesos per kilometer of track.[2]

The railroad's approval by the federal government was an experiment for Mexico, and the young Díaz government provided specific and unique guidelines about the rights and limitations of the newly formed company. Article II of Chapter II of the contract between the government and the company prescribed: "The enterprise shall always be Mexican, even when all or any of its members are foreigners."[3] This simple affirmation of Mexican nationalism and ownership would have enormous repercussions for Mexico and for the railroad in subsequent decades. This Mexican desire to maintain sovereignty ran directly in the face of such attitudes as that of W. R. Morley, whom the AT&SF had instructed to find the best route to the ocean west from Arizona. Morley noted that creating a rail link into Mexico would "bring Adventurers, who will persistently work for, and finally succeed in obtaining another 'Texas' from the Territory of Old Mexico."[4]

By 1880, the AT&SF had begun construction on the line, starting at Nogales, Arizona. The company reached Guaymas by the end of 1882, and the railroad was off and running. The line gave Mexico a convenient link from port to border and provided both the government and the railroad with revenue from freight and passengers. But although the Sonora Railway turned a small profit during its seventeen years under AT&SF ownership, the railroad did not make the money company executives had hoped for. The line shipped a variety of items while owned by the AT&SF, including beer from Anheuser Busch into Mexico and cattle out of Mexico, as well as other foodstuffs, cloth, and raw agricultural goods.[5] But demand did not remain steady enough for the owners' satisfaction, and the line did not connect to the more populated regions of Mexico. Freight traveling south of Guaymas had to go by oxencart over land or by ship along the coast to be sent inland from Acapulco. Furthermore, the lucrative mining areas were not close enough to the railroad's right-of-way to allow the line to tap into mining and ore shipments.

Many people had high hopes for the railroad. In describing its place in the Sonoran landscape, one writer expressed the hopes of many for the railroad—hopes that would live on for decades: "The establishment of a railroad line has opened fertile horizons to two of the most powerful elements of the state: the minerals, that have nourished so much we covet, and have given Sonora for years before a nearly mythological name; and agriculture, which is the true center of its wealth."[6]

The government carefully regulated the new line. Mexico burdened the Sonora Railway with heavy tariffs on certain goods, so that the company was required to ship certain items by different classes and to pay tariffs depending on the class of good being shipped. Tariff lists produced by the railroad categorized every conceivable good via a bewildering classification system. For instance, the railroad had to ship shovels, ammonia, saffron, and starch first-class, costing the company a higher amount in tariffs, while alum, cannon balls, and coffins had second-class status, and roofing materials, anchors, manure, and adobe bricks went third-class.[7]

The AT&SF had also never been happy with the port of Guaymas, because its sparse harbor facilities could not accommodate large ships. By 1897, the AT&SF had become interested in divesting the Guaymas-Nogales railroad in exchange for another line—one of the SP's routes, which ran from the Mojave Desert to Needles in the United States. Because the SP was just starting to consider expanding into Mexico, it expressed interest in the Sonora Railway. The two organizations agreed upon a reciprocal trade in 1897.

Díaz found the arrangement more than acceptable. The SP was better-financed than the AT&SF and had a better track record in completing and operating profitable routes in the United States. On July 15, 1898, under the terms of the reciprocal lease, the SP assumed operation of the Sonora Railway. The face value of the line at the time was 5,248,000 pesos, along with an additional par value of stock totalling another 1,049,000 pesos.[8]

Until 1898, Mexico had entertained little serious thought of extending the line south of Guaymas, despite considerable discussion within government circles about the desirability of doing so. Attitudes began to change as the century drew to a close, though, and in 1898 and 1905 a group of men converged in a series of meetings that would lead to a decision to expand the line down to Guadalajara. The four parts of the equation consisted of General Luis Torres, a close friend of Díaz and a former governor of the state of Sinaloa; SP President Collis P. Huntington; his successor, Edward H. Harriman; and SP administrator Julius Kruttschnitt.

In 1898, and then again in 1900, General Torres held lengthy discussions in Hermosillo with Huntington and Kruttschnitt about the possibility of expanding the line southward. It had been Díaz' wish to have Torres broach these discussions, and don Porfirio was extremely anxious to have Huntington make a firm commitment to extend the line to the south in order to meet with the northern terminus of a line running from Mexico City to Guadalajara. It was a top priority of Díaz and his Minister of Public Works, Leandro Fernández, to have a connection made by rail between northern and southern Mexico. Earlier offers of concessions to other concerns had proved fruitless, but Díaz considered the SP's large size and great success in U.S. railroading circles the best opportunity yet to obtain a line all the way down the west coast. He thus pressed with extra vigor to get the SP to commit to the work.[9]

Díaz had several motivations to build the line. Although he and the científicos recognized the commercial value in completing such a line, the government also had strong military concerns: they had no way to get soldiers from the capital to the west coast of Mexico—a vital concern for Díaz in his otherwise tightly controlled empire. And national pride, boosted for many years by the legends of Mexican military successes at Puebla, Veracruz, the Alamo, and the Goliad and stung by military failure during the Mexican-American War, often became focused tightly on issues of national defense. Events far from Mexico City, such as the sporadic Yaqui raids in the Yaqui River and the Cananea labor strike of 1907, alarmed Díaz and reinforced his belief in the need for tight military control of the country.[10]

One of the complexities of the military as a contributor to Mexican nationbuilding is that it provided cohesiveness through conflict, as did so many other strains of Mexican nationalism. The combination of the railroad and the military provided dramatic images well suited to the country's sense of purpose and pride: the snorting, stomping locomotive; the snap and polish of military exercises along the line; and the notions of protection, might, and machismo.

Meanwhile, Huntington was interested in expanding into Mexico. However, he had not fully made up his mind to do so, was preoccupied with business dealings elsewhere in the United States, and would not commit to undertake the construction. Torres approached the U.S. railroad magnate in 1898 and again in 1900 but was unable to secure a promise from Huntington to expand the line southward. So the line continued its modestly profitable operations between Guaymas and Nogales, and no further discussions took place between Mexico City leaders and SP officials for the next four years.

But the seed was planted, and in 1904, Mr. J. A. Naugle, assistant general manager for the SP, was in Mexico City procuring a concession for the Inter-California Railway, an SP railroad subsidiary in Baja California. Fernández (who would later serve as head of the Communications and Public Works Department during Díaz' last four years, overseeing the nation's railroads) approached Naugle and told him that the government would grant 20,000 pesos per kilometer, payable in gold, to any "reliable party" willing to connect the Sonora Railway with the MCR—good money, when Mexican railroad concessions had been averaging 8,935 pesos per kilometer. (Generous though Mexican railway subsidies may have seemed, they were nevertheless half the average subsidy given in Chile at the time, and a third of the subsidies given in the Argentine Republic.)[11]

Harriman, who had replaced Huntington as the president of the SP after the latter's death in late 1900, finally instructed Kruttschnitt in 1905 to take steps to get the concession. The hard-working and extremely effective Kruttschnitt, the highest-paid railroad executive in the world by the 1920s,[12] was "a ruddy-faced man of great bulk and slow movements" and apparently "had absolutely no imagination. His implements were facts; he was a living index of railroad facts." He was, noted his fellow railroad director Frank Vanderlip, the man who kept Harriman's railroads in tune. "He was not a man to let enthusiasm run away with his judgment, and that was something that made him a perfect complement of E. H. Harriman."[13] Kruttschnitt, the passionateless railroad magnate, contrasted sharply with fiery and outspoken Mexican railroad men like Alberto J. Pani. By 1905, Kruttschnitt was committed to getting the concession, and ordered Naugle to take steps to do so.

Naugle, acting as the SP's foot soldier in Mexico City, after further discussions with Fernández, Vice President Ramón Corral, and others, secured the concession. Another U.S. firm had offered to construct the line for five million pesos less, but President Díaz and his ministers preferred giving the concession to the SP even at the increased price. However, Díaz and his cabinet insisted strongly that work should be begun promptly and finished in reasonable time.[14]

On August 14, 1905, Fernández signed the concession with Naugle; by then the subsidy had risen yet another 500 pesos, for a total subsidy of 12,500 pesos per kilometer, to "construct and exploit" about 1,247 kilometers of railroad from a point near Guaymas, generally down along the west coast but also including the towns of Culiacán, Mazatlán, Santiago, and Tepic, and joining up at "the most convenient" point on the MCR between San Marcos and Guadalajara. The government also made a deposit of 240,000 pesos' worth of government bonds to guarantee fulfillment of the obligation.[15]

The government very carefully circumscribed the railroad's obligations and rights for the extension of the line. Fernandez oversaw the creation of a contract stipulating hundreds of different elements of the railroad's daily operations. Government leaders had a clear vision of the degree of control they wished to exert over the railroad, and the lengthy series of contracts between the government and the railroad show this vision clearly. The contracts spelled out basic items such as freight and passenger rates and included such details as allowable items for importation, storage rates, cost for telegrams sent by the railroad along company-owned wires, and more. The contracts also referred explicitly to the 1899 Railroad Law.

Díaz' vision of a line from northernmost Mexico down to Guadalajara and thence to Mexico City was quickly becoming a reality, and work proceeded from both ends of the route: from Guaymas southward along the rich coastal plains of Sinaloa below Mazatlán, and north from Tequila in the high country of Jalisco. The company broke ground at Empalme in late August 1905, and by 1906, rapid progress began. The first several years of construction moved swiftly because of the flat terrain south of Guaymas and the relatively stable political status of Mexico.

The 103 kilometers from Empalme to Corral opened to traffic in July 1906, the 43-kilometer stretch between Corral and Velderrain opened in February 1907, and the 43 kilometers to Navojoa opened in May 1907. On June 24, 1909, confident of a bright future in Mexico, the

SP incorporated the railroad as the SP de Mex. The bulk of the line—more than 90 percent—had been completed by 1911 from Nogales down to Tepic, leaving the 103-mile stretch through the rugged mountains of the barrancas region. By 1909, the government was thoroughly convinced that the SP de Mex—also frequently referred to as the "Ferrocarril Alamos-Guadalajara" in Mexican documentary sources—was the company best suited to tie northwestern Mexico to the heavily populated south. The government was motivated by economic as well as political and military reasons. While gold and silver ore had issued forth from mines on the Mexican west coast since the colonial era, Mexico now felt poised to extract a new kind of gold, in the form of produce grown in the rich coastal soil of Sinaloa. Noted one official in Empalme to the central government: "A great impulse will now be unfurled: above all, agriculture has taken, and continues to take, flight, in a manner that gives room for the exportation of innumerable quantities of garbanzos, tomatoes, oranges, melons, watermelons, onions, peppers and other products of this rich land—products that had never previously been considered for extraction."[16]

The Mexican government was also impressed by the SP's size and power, by its organization and engineering ability, and by its reputation. And to SP officials like Huntington, Harriman, and Epes Randolph, Latin America offered new frontiers to conquer. The desires of Mexican government leaders and railroad administrators dovetailed neatly—or so it seemed.

SP Attitudes Towards Mexico

But SP perceptions of Mexico differed greatly from the actual political and social milieu of the country. Huntington had made money in the western United States by pushing lines into new and "unconquered" territory, and he believed that expansion into Mexico would earn healthy profits. Huntington also had other Latin American transportation properties. He was an owner of the Pacific Improvement Company, which held title to a proposed railroad in Guatemala. He had a part interest in the United States and Brazil Steamship Company and also controlled the Mexican International Railway as early as the 1880s.

Huntington's paternalistic attitude towards Latin America exemplified the views of many foreign investors in the region. Speaking in March 1900 to the Galveston, Texas Chamber of Commerce, just months before his death, Huntington remarked: "All the islands that we have taken we must keep, and deal with their people firmly but kindly, so that they will not only love but respect us."[17] This contradictory attitude of "conquest and love" was common among some U.S. participants in Latin America. They believed not only that the United States was qualified to manage the affairs of other countries outside of its borders, but that the populations of those countries would welcome U.S. involvement.

Huntington employee and SP de Mex President Epes Randolph's attitudes about expansion into Mexico reinforced and confirmed Huntington's attitudes. The SP planned to lead the way into Mexico by steel rail and steam locomotive. Some company officials viewed Mexico as an extension of the United States. As Randolph would crow near the close of the military hostilities of the Mexican Revolution, "The West Coast of Mexico will be the new Southern California!"[18]

Randolph and other SP de Mex officials occasionally expressed sentiments about "Americanizing" Mexico. And U.S. soldiers and filibusterers from the Mexican-American War to the Mexican Revolution had expressed the view that the United States should and could "conquer," "overcome," and "win" Mexico. But the United States could not do so via the Mexican west coast, because before 1927 the SP de Mex could not yet provide a far western U.S. connection to central Mexico by rail. Nor could Mexico fully realize national unity in the ways that a completed line would allow: the ability to move troops by rail to the west coast; the means to provide transportation to Mexico City for the numerous northwestern communities through which the railroad passed; or the ability to aid economic development by exporting goods from along the coast into the United States. As the Porfiriato ended, the relationship between Díaz' empire and the railroad thus consisted of half-assembled parts: a railroad not quite completed; a government not quite convinced of the surety of its steps towards railroad nationalization; and a científico group whose influence had been undercut by growing discontent over Díaz' regime.

The government's interactions with the railroad changed form during the revolution. The wide-ranging influence of Positivism ebbed as the chaos of the conflict invalidated philosophies of order and progress, and científico-inspired expressions of what the nation needed were replaced by attitudes that effectively negated a number of the line's desires and abilities. The federal government's first change of approach was to ignore the railroad altogether, leaving it to fend largely for itself during the conflict.

The Revolution and the Railroad

The timing of the start of the Mexican Revolution could not have been worse for the SP de Mex or for the SP. In 1910, the SP had given its newly incorporated subsidiary in Mexico more than $38 million U.S. so that construction of the line southward from Guaymas and northward from Guadalajara could begin in earnest. However, a substantial amount of that money was spent during the next decade just to repair damaged bridges and trackage and to replace destroyed cars and engines.

The most difficult years for the SP de Mex, both militarily and in terms of physical disruption of the line and its accompanying inability to serve various locales, spanned the five years from 1912 to 1916. The line did not feel the actual impact of the conflict until April 1911, when fierce fighting and sporadic vandalism reduced a number of bridges and trestles to rubble in the state of Sinaloa. The 1911 annual report of the SP noted that "during the month of May [1911], the interruptions from this cause were so frequent that the traffic over the line was practically suspended."[19] That year, the company pushed on doggedly but managed to build only 20.4 kilometers of track. The year 1912 was not much better; a total of only 50.2 kilometers was constructed between Mazatlán and Tepic. Even those hard-won kilometers of construction were eroded when rebels burned twenty-seven wooden trestles between February and June of 1912.

Once Victoriano Huerta took power in early 1913, actual construction work on the SP de Mex line shuddered to a complete halt. The company had hoped that Huerta might signal a return to some of the economic stability enjoyed by U.S. businesses in Mexico during the Porfiriato. But this was not to be the case. By mid-1914, the company estimated its losses for the year at approximately eight million pesos.

Within six weeks of coming to power, Huerta himself asked both the U.S. State Department and the SP for help in constructing new rails. Some of the requested work involved the SP de Mex lines; other work involved building new sections of railroad passing through Chihuahua and Sonora. Huerta primarily wanted to be able to mobilize troops in these northwestern states and offered to provide the SP de Mex with several thousand soldiers to "protect" the SP de Mex line and to do construction work on these projects. Despite the vaguely ominous tone of Huerta's request, the SP de Mex turned him down.

But life near the border, where the SP de Mex was still struggling to extract the most value from the copper fields in Cananea through their recently purchased subsidiary, the Cananea, Río Yaquí y Pacifico, was made particularly difficult not only by Huerta's actions but by reactions to Huerta as well. As he systematically harassed the U.S. copper companies in the region, Huerta also forced the SP de Mex to suspend operations completely in the state. On March 5, 1913, the state of Sonora officially refused to recognize Huerta's regime, and Sonoran troops moved against the Huertistas the next day, burning the bridges between Hermosillo and Guaymas in order to prevent the federals from moving north of Guaymas.

The young Sonoran cavalry commander, Alvaro Obregón, slowly worked his way northward. Intent on reaching Nogales to render aid, he had his troops rebuild the bridges until they had exhausted the supply of wood available for construction. He then marched into Nogales rather than wait for more timber. The SP de Mex found itself not only incapable of operating the line but also unable to prevent destruction or to work on reconstruction during the spring of 1913.[20]

All was not complete anarchy during the terms of the *roi du jour* in power in Mexico during the 1913–1916 period, however. The company earned some government revenues from the transportation of troops and war munitions. But the railroad unsuccessfully charged another 1.85 million pesos to the Mexican government for troop train service and for road "rental" (the SP de Mex's euphemistic term for government cooption of the line by revolutionary troops)—a bill that remained unpaid by the end of 1914.[21]

In the face of the revolution, the company had to realign its expectations, and "success" for the SP de Mex came to mean simply being able to run trains as close to schedule as possible and with as much order as possible. Huerta had not deeply entrenched himself enough to wield administrative or legal power to get the SP de Mex's attention, but he did manage to instead use military force to control the railroad's operations to some degree.

The independent SP de Mex suffered considerably more than the Mexican and U.S. lines under the National Railways of Mexico (NRM; Ferrocarriles Nacionales de México), whose operations remained profitable and consistent until 1915. The reasons for the discrepancy between the SP de Mex's 1912–1916 operational difficulties and the NRM's relative successes remain somewhat speculative. Part of the reason probably lay in the disproportionate number of physical attacks the line suffered due to its U.S. ownership, while the national lines maintained an aura of pride for Mexicans of all social and economic strata and thus suffered fewer depredations. The SP de Mex was also trying to operate a new railroad from its headquarters in Tucson, with a new staff pulled from different regions of the United States, most with no experience in Mexican railroading. The NRM, while also only recently formed, was at least manned with personnel with many years' experience in Mexican railroad circles. In any case, once Venustiano Carranza had a sufficient grasp upon power in Mexico by the end of 1916 and was able to call the constitutional convention that would assemble in 1917, the effect of military disruption upon the railroad eased considerably.

However, military chaos was replaced by a lack of administrative interest in the line by the Carranza government and this lack of government supervision, which *prima facie* should have given the railroad more operational freedom, turned out to have a more detrimental effect on the SP de Mex than the previous warfare of 1912–1916 had. As early as December 1914, even before he had sufficiently consolidated power to effectively do so, Carranza attempted to regulate Mexican railroads. He issued a memorandum regarding the takeover of the NRM, and in it he specifically excluded the SP de Mex's line—"which has always been managed by its own administration," he noted.[22] The railroad suffered fewer financial losses due to destruction of property after 1916, but it was expected to operate almost completely independently. Carranza's regime remained sympathetic but unsupportive of the railroad. In late 1916, E. Coretta, the Department of Communications and Public Works's (SCOP; Secretaría de Comunicaciones y Obras Públicas) chief of railroad inspection, noted:

> The abnormal conditions during the Revolution have deeply affected traffic on the SP's line, so that only military transportation has been allowed, and generally occupies the line. At the same time, construction has been suspended, with only the most critical elements warranting repair. . . . the rains have caused landslides, collapses, uneven terrain for building, and rotting of railroad ties. And the company has evidently not had the time to make repairs along these notoriously deteriorated stretches.[23]

Although agreeing that the railroad had a tremendous stake in increasing traffic along the line, the government equated "acts of war" to "acts of nature." Just as the rains were not the fault of the Mexican government, neither were depredations from the revolution truly its responsibility.

Mexican transportation officials also felt strongly and consistently that the SP de Mex's size and experience were reason enough to deny further assistance to the company. "The company has a solid foundation for success, and there is no urgency that justifies a quick inspection of their lines. We can reverify this issue during the course of next year (1917)," remarked Coretta.[24] He continued, "We must bear in mind that conditions in the country may now permit us to deal with the issue of reparations and resume the construction work [to finish the line], but we know that the company is neither stubborn nor tardy in its activities."

The SP's very bigness and past success meant that it had to stand on its own. However, although the government may have rendered virtually no aid to the railroad, it watched the company closely. "It is the principal point of the Law [of 1899] to watch over the financial state of the [SP de Mex] railroad company," noted Coretta in a 1917 memo:

> The Inspector will make the basis of his work the gathering of necessary data that contains the following: the numbers and residences of the functionaries and higher employees of the Company; the dividends paid to and by the Company; the types of actions taken, their natures, if they are ordinary or extraordinary, etc.; their consolidated and floating debt, distinguishing among the different types; the interest paid for each type; the description of the line; the original cost of constructing the line . . .[25]

The government also resented what it perceived as arrogance on the part of the railroad. Carrancista officials found the SP de Mex's own aloofness towards the government during the revolution frustrating and responded in kind. "The SP for some time has kept to itself," wrote Coretta to the head of the SCOP, "and due to the current conditions, we feel no obligation to [help them by inspecting the line]."[26] The government provided lines under the NRM umbrella with considerable technical and administrative support but simultaneously refused to assist the SP de Mex during the conflict. But the government's unwillingness to extend a helping hand to the railroad did not stem from carelessness or distraction. In fact, the government watched the SP de Mex extremely closely, generating report after report on its financial, engineering, and staffing status.[27]

Throughout the revolution, both government and railroad held considerable misconceptions about the needs and motivations of the other. For their part, SP de Mex officials equated revolution with an inability to self-govern: "Just now I do not see any likelihood of peace —in fact it is my own opinion that none of us will ever see Mexico again governed by Mexicans," noted Randolph in July 1913.[28] The government incorrectly assumed the railroad was too large and self-sufficient to truly need scarce Mexican manpower, and the railroad incorrectly assumed the government was unable to effectively regulate railroad activities within the country because of the scale of the conflict and the accompanying chaos. In fact, the government's operation of the NRM had been financially successful well into 1914, and the renamed National Constitutional Railroads (NCR; Ferrocarriles Constitucionalistas de México) had then been carefully regulated during Carranza's rule.

Carranza government officials made it clear in their internal correspondence that they were willing to use the leverage of possible concessions as another reason to delay giving the SP de Mex a wider variety of support during the last years of the revolution and, for that specific reason, withheld aid in track inspection, technical assistance with line rebuilding, and more. Railroad manpower was also in very short supply during the conflict, and the much larger NRM rail network took up a correspondingly larger amount of the SCOP's time. The NRM lines thus experienced correspondingly better financial performance.

By early 1917, as widespread fighting had eased and the constitutional convention convened in Querétaro, SP de Mex executives felt new hopes for greater attention from the government or, at the very least, a broaching of the issues of reparations and renewed construction. A new constitution, they reasoned, would bring a degree of order to Mexico that would greatly facilitate railroad growth. However, the 1917 Mexican Constitution—the very document that provided a measure of stability for Mexico after the revolution—would prove highly disruptive to foreign railroad operations in Mexico: in particular, the creation of Article 123 of the Mexican Constitution would haunt the SP de Mex in at least two ways.

First, Article 123 stipulated specifically that all railroad structures in the country be permanent within ten years. This was important from a cost standpoint, because SP de Mex officials made it clear that their own plans to modernize the line would take considerably longer than a decade, if they were allowed to have their way. The issue of improvements also became a major bone of contention between the SP de Mex and the Mexican government in the early 1920s once the railroad and the government entered into discussions to resume construction. The law ultimately forced the SP de Mex to make improvements it considered either premature or, worse, totally unnecessary in some cases. Second, future Mexican presidents would use Article 123 for land appropriation on a vast scale, which directly affected the lands through which the railroads passed and thus their ownership and control over those agriculturally important lands.

Again, the SP found itself in a situation diametrically opposed to what it was used to in the United States, where large railroads controlled land by the millions of acres. In Mexico during and after the revolution, Article 123 created a climate unfavorable to foreign railroad efforts to use Mexican lands for railroad buildings, spurs, or other purposes. Mexican law, complementing the country's populist land reform spirit, gave the government control over Mexican land while firmly and explicitly denying assistance to the SP de Mex. And when the railroad attempted to use Mexican law to its advantage, it often ran into resistance—as exemplified by the issue of reparations.

Negotiations, Reparations, and Agreement

Railroad officials began presenting claims to the Mexican government almost immediately after receiving word of damages to track and structures in 1911. But restitution did not come quickly or easily. Over the next ten years, railroad officials brought claims aggregating twenty-two million pesos against the Mexican government for damages by both federal and rebel forces, charges for transporting troops and supplies, and rental of company property—steadily increasing dollar amounts that the SP faithfully chronicled each year and which are echoed in Mexican documentary sources.[29] The SP de Mex kept its own detailed listings of what equipment and buildings had been destroyed during the conflict, ranging from a twenty-peso amount for rock, up to a bridge valued at fifteen thousand pesos destroyed near Nogales in 1914.[30]

In 1917, Carranza established a commission to study these and other claims—the Revision Commission for Reclamations to the Southern Pacific of Mexico Railroad (Comisión Revisora de Reclamaciones del Ferrocarril Sud-Pacífico de México), based in Mazatlán.[31] But again his government did nothing, neither publishing nor announcing the results of the commission's work. A large part of the problem lay in conflicting perceptions of fairness, justice, and responsibility. Both the government and the railroad strongly desired to complete the line southward to Guadalajara so it could connect from there to the NRM line running into Mexico City. Neither side questioned the efficacy and necessity of completing the line. Driven by the concerns of bottom-line-oriented administrators and pressure from the SP, the SP de Mex wanted repayment for what it considered unfair destruction of its property—destruction it believed the government had a clear obligation to recompense.

But Mexican leaders felt no strong responsibility to make reparations for actions out of their control. The above-mentioned issues of bigness and aloofness also dulled Mexican desires to assist the railroad. If the government and the railroad had experienced so little interaction during the conflict, and the railroad had not complained, why should the government suddenly have an obligation to now help the railroad in the form of reparations? Furthermore, Mexican payments to a foreign railroad over damages suffered in a national conflict marked by the deaths of many Mexicans—and virtually no Americans—would serve as an affront to Mexican nationalism.

Negotiations after the revolution remained at a standstill until 1921. The government consistently stalled the SP de Mex, not turning its attention to reparations until Obregón had been in office for several months. The issue of the reparations themselves would also have been straightforward had it not been complicated by the issue of concessions. In 1921, the SP de Mex submitted claims totaling more than thirty-two million pesos. This bill included slightly less than ten million pesos that the SP de Mex claimed the government owed it on account of nonpayment of subsidies.

The Mexican government responded that the completed sections of track contained a number of structures characterized as "temporary" by the government's inspectors, and thus the government did not owe any subsidy to the SP de Mex until the company had replaced those structures with permanent structures. To further complicate matters, Article 123, in its section requiring all railroad structures to be permanent within ten years, did not specify exactly what would happen to U.S. companies if those structures were not made permanent, nor did its language spell out just what constituted "permanent."

The rest of the reparations money—twenty-two million pesos—

claimed by the SP de Mex was for damages by both federal and rebel forces to the line, charges for transporting troops and supplies, and rental of company property. The issue of precisely how the Mexican government would repay the railroad arose again and again. Mexico wanted to complete the line but begged poverty; Obregón claimed that the money simply did not exist.[32] Payment to the railroad in the form of government bonds was the only financial incentive Mexico was willing to offer. E. R. Jones, the president of Wells Fargo of Mexico, wrote to SP President Harvey B. Titcomb in late December of 1921 and remarked plaintively that "[Obregón] realizes and appreciates that this will give a lot of work to Mexican people who really need the help, and if you can come down here with some plan that does not require a present outlay of money by the Government you can get by immediately, but if the plan requires a present outlay of money my belief is that you will have to wait."[33]

But the railroad could not afford to wait much longer to resolve the issue because it was operating a partial line with no southern terminus—and losing money in the process. The company was eager to begin work. "The acreage and possibilities are so great that an empire could be fed from this soil," noted Titcomb to Kruttschnitt in the fall of 1921.[34] But the railroad was also motivated by a fear of competition and wary of calling the Mexican government's bluff regarding the upgrading of the line and buildings to "permanent" status. For example, Titcomb noted in a 1922 letter to SP Chairman Kruttschnitt:

> We cannot rely too strongly or too fully upon justice of the law in Mexico, and it may be that it is possible that the Tonichi Branch may be confiscated by the Government on account of non-operation. Our claims account of depredations are too apt to be set aside by the Federal Government under one pretext or another. . . . we do have the antagonism to some extent of president Obregón, and undoubtedly he leans to the construction of the line by [the National Railways].[35]

Titcomb also made detailed suggestions for 7,2275,000 pesos in improvements by the SP in order to placate the Mexican government. Apparently the railroad made many, although not all, of those improvements. One stimulus may have been a letter from Obregón himself, dated May 31, 1922. Obregón, who hailed from the city of Navojoa in Sonora and who owned thousands of acres of vegetable-producing land there, suggested that it would be "opportune" for the SP de Mex to start work on the neglected Tonichi Branch, adding that "it would be greatly pleasing to know that the work in question would start in the near future."[36]

Obregón also contemplated having the NRM finish the line, but others in his government opposed such a scheme. Roberto Pesquiera, director of the NRM, acted as perhaps the strongest advocate of having the SP de Mex complete the segment.[37] Pesquiera reportedly remarked to Obregón, when pressed on the issue, that it made no sense to have the government undertake the costly and very heavy construction and be forced to handle the freight over the most difficult part of the line.

But although Mexico decided not to complete the line itself, the country's leaders manifested a serious, "do-it-ourselves" spirit as they contemplated completion of the line. This sentiment manifested itself clearly and loudly enough for the SP de Mex to launch a series of studies comparing its proposed route from Tepic to La Quemada across the barrancas region with a route proposed by the government from Tepic to San Marcos. Comparing the NRM's proposed route to its own, the company found that the amount specified in construction estimates by the NRM were too low by about 50 percent. This simply meant that the NRM thought that it could construct the line for less than the SP felt was possible. The SP de Mex concluded that its planned line was the best located, shortest, most economical to operate, and would in actuality not exceed the cost of any other proposed line.[38]

In ultimately favoring the SP de Mex as the company best suited to complete the line, Mexico had to sort through many interests from around the globe that wanted to develop competing sections of track in Mexico—particularly in the state of Sonora—in the relatively stable years after 1920. A German company expressed interest in constructing a line from the port of Huatabampo into the Yaqui Valley. The El Paso & Southwestern Railroad studied the possibility of constructing a line from the end of the Nacozari Railroad to the coast (fig. 3.2). The

3.2 Loading baggage onto a Ferrocarril de Nacozari passenger car. The Nacozari spur line, operated by the Southern Pacific, moved both mining ore and passengers along its route. The ore was being shipped from the Sierra Madre mining center of Nacozari and consisted of copper, gold, silver, and manganese. (Courtesy of Donald Duke, Golden West Books, San Marino, California)

Phelps-Dodge interests, prominent in U.S. railroading, continued to push for potential expansion of their own line south of Nacozari. The Foundation Company, a New York–based firm with offices in Mexico, offered to build the line for cost plus 25 percent. The latter was the most serious competitor to the SP, having "lots of money and . . . certainly in the good graces of president Obregón."[39]

But the government ultimately rejected all companies except the SP de Mex as suitors for construction of the country's west coast line. The railroad was a known quantity to the government. The company had proved pliant in the face of Mexican desires to maintain administrative control over the line in the past. And the SP's technical skills and persistence were already legendary as a result of the company's construction of the transcontinental line in the United States a half-century earlier and its subsequent commercial successes. To Mexican government leaders, completion of the line by the company was a near certainty. The SP de Mex had built the rest of the line and knew the route intimately, leading government officials to conclude that it had a much higher chance at forging a rail link from north to south than any other bidder.

In coming to agreement in 1922 and 1923, the government and the railroad reached several compromises. The Mexican government allowed the "temporary" structures to be upgraded to more permanent ones over several years, resolving that particular issue. Additionally, the Mexican government firmly decided against itself taking on construction of the line through the barrancas region, feeling that the cost and difficulty were best borne by an external source.[40] Having a foreign company complete the line also precluded the possibility of government embarrassment if the construction work ran into any major delays or cost overruns. If necessary, the SP de Mex could be pointed to as a failed U.S. endeavor, which the press, which closely watched the proceedings, could then tout as a victory of nature over man—in particular, Mexican nature over U.S. man.

The government also agreed to pay the SP de Mex the full amount requested: a sum of 23,202,261.79 pesos in the form of forty equal payments of Mexican government notes, with maturation taking place between 1923 and 1931. Railroad officials were satisfied with this sum and had not expected much more in the way of a settlement. As SP executive Kruttschnitt wrote to Titcomb in late 1922, "The point I wish to make to you confidentially is that if we get somewhere between 25,000,000 and 27,000,000 pesos as they stand to date, we will be very lucky."[41]

Obregón also agreed to amend the original concessions in various ways, including the elimination of the period between 1911 and 1923 in calculating the ninety-nine-year life of the original concession. The SP de Mex agreed to rehabilitate the Tonichi and Los Alamos branch lines within two years, as well as complete the unfinished portion of the line.[42]

With exceptionally careful timing, the government then waited until only six weeks from completion of the agreement to flick a new fly into the ointment. At the start of the year, the *Diario Oficial* decreed that government would levy a tax of 10 percent on the gross income of railroads operating in Mexico.[43] The executive order, by Obregón, noted that all companies, domestic or foreign, would pay the tax "upon the value of the payments which the public services of the railroads require for passages, freights, storages, deliveries, telegrams, and whatever else they collect by reason of the exploitation."

This not only let the government generate revenue from the railroad, but also allowed Mexican officials to gain much greater knowledge of the company's business operations. Railroads had to submit detailed financial statements to the government as well as pay the tax. This element did not appear of great import to the SP de Mex in 1923; the potential loss of revenue and privacy seemed small compared to the increase in potential earnings and the chance, finally, to receive reparations for revolutionary depredations. But the requirement to pay the 10 percent tax would increasingly frustrate the railroad as the years passed and other obstacles appeared.

In deciding to continue with the line, the SP de Mex also had tenacity and the perhaps regrettable momentum of substantial prior investment: by the spring of 1922, the company had invested a total of $42,889,538 U.S. in the road, equipment, and miscellaneous physical property associated with the line—and it was not about to let that very large investment go to waste.[44] The SP also owned a company called the East Coast Oil Company that regularly produced five thousand gallons of oil a day from one well, which was used by the SP de Mex for its own fuel purposes, but that was thought at the time to hold far larger untapped reserves. This oil issue was especially important for Mexico, which had high hopes for oil production in the 1920s.[45]

The government and the railroad executed the final agreement on March 2, 1923, and both sides felt they had gained the better of the other. From the government's perspective, the reparations provided Mexico City with a relatively affordable link to the northwest, a chance to have some form of control over Sonoran and northwestern affairs, the benefit of reaping profits from the 10 percent tax, and an opportunity to use the railroad as a symbol of Mexican unity—very important to the government after the recent divisiveness of the revolution. Although it would have to pay several million pesos in reparations, the government would not have to invest national funds in construction itself. A foreign company would complete the line through an almost unimaginably difficult section: the barrancas region, a rugged twenty-five-kilometer stretch of terrain marked by deep gorges, wide rivers, and crumbling rock. The signed agreement provided useful fodder for Obregón, who used it to help secure what one U.S. newspaper called the "virtual business recognition of President Obregón."[46]

The idea of a burgeoning Pan-American "friendship" between the two countries also appeared repeatedly, despite the fact that the arrangement was strictly for business purposes. Titcomb noted the day after the agreement was signed that "Mr. de la Huerta, Secretary of Finance and Public Credit. . . . stated plainly and earnestly that the S.P. de M. had demonstrated its friendship in the fullest manner to the republic. President Obregón states that this act gives him great satisfaction, as it was constructive work so necessary for the development of Mexico."[47]

It was also constructive work that Obregón wanted done for his own personal gain. His properties in Yavarro and elsewhere in Sonora benefited directly from SP de Mex's harbor dredging, spur building, and other activities in the state.

But in the SP's view, the railroad had gained the best part of the bargain via the agreement. Its claims against the government would be settled and a handsome amount of money paid them over time. Tourism could be stimulated along the Mexican west coast, and the SP de Mex would please its own supporters in the U.S. government. The agreement also satisfied the U.S. State Department, particularly because the line could stimulate mining, which would benefit the United States in several ways—financially, for the private corporations involved, but also because it provided a potential steady nearby source of copper and steel. Both commodities had been in short supply during World War I.

SP de Mex officials also showed a new attitude about markets.

Railroad administrators appear to have been less concerned in 1922 about serving U.S. markets than they were about getting lucrative produce from the rich western lands in Sonora and Sinaloa down into Mexico City. As the only line running through this rich agricultural area, the SP de Mex had the potential to serve all of Mexico City with fruits, vegetables, and other farm products. As the company noted in 1922:

> The country through which the line already operates is susceptible of greatly increased production, but a number of its products are the same as produced in the United States, and the duties and other restrictions imposed upon imports from Mexico limit the available markets [in the United States] for the Mexican products . . . on the other hand the present termination of the Mexican line at Tepic affords no outlet for these products to the consuming markets of the Republic of Mexico. The proposed completion of the line to a connection with the National Railways . . . will give these products access to the Mexican consuming markets . . .[48]

The directors of the SP, carefully eyeing their Mexican line, felt confident that there was money to be made south of the U.S. border— confident enough that they appeared satisfied, charitable, and almost jubilant upon the conclusion of the agreement. "Your Directors consider the settlement of issues with the Mexican Government, which met your representatives in a fair and broad spirit, a favorable one both for our Sister Republic and your Mexican property," administrators noted as they addressed their stockholders in 1922. At last, they thought, their costly Mexican experiment would begin to pay some dividends. SP railroad administrators now felt that Mexico was a "sister republic" and not the country they had previously called "ungovernable."

Resumption of Construction

Although the line had been 90 percent completed for more than a decade, in many ways the ceremony marking resumption of construction was similar to that held for the start of an entirely new railroad. And in some ways, the company was starting a new railroad. Completion of the line through to Guadalajara would finally tie northern Mexico directly to Mexico City by rail. By 1923, Mexico had changed remarkably from 1909. Díaz was dead, Positivism was no longer a discernible element of national identity, José Yves Limantour was exiled overseas, and Mexican attitudes towards the SP de Mex had taken new directions.

The extravagant 1923 ceremony reflected Mexican and U.S. attitudes that the line was new. Perhaps never before in the history of railroading has the resumption of existing construction been marked with such fanfare. A gigantic marching band played, and leaders from both countries hosted a lavish banquet with flowing champagne. Dozens of national and international reporters covered the festivities. President Obregón gave a lengthy speech, as did several SP representatives, including Kruttschnitt, along with Harry Chandler, publisher of the *Los Angeles Times*. The texts of the speeches given at the ceremony reflect the distinct differences in attitudes towards Mexican control of the line. Chandler gave his talk first, noting:

> The fact that the financial interests which are behind the Southern Pacific Railroad Company of Mexico, one of the most powerful railroad enterprises in the world, is willing to come here and invest millions upon millions in this important project, will serve to convince the entire world, as nothing else would at this time, that there is a sincere and constructive patriotism in the hearts of those persons who are directing the destinies of Mexico.

In thus attributing nationalist spirit and patriotism to the Mexican people, Chandler implied that, somehow, foreign monies being spent in Mexico were supposed to bring a swell of pride to Mexico, rather than pride generated by some other, more internal impetus. However, Chandler had the equation backwards, as Obregón's speech next indicated: "Mexico is not a country opposed to civilization; but it does oppose and shall oppose the imposition of a certain kind of civilization. . . . My message, I hope, may reach all the people in the United States, that is: 'Order has come out of chaos'; 'deal fairly with the Mexican Government in a spirit of fairness and you will be received and dealt with fairly.'"

Obregón, while espousing the benefits of progress and "order," made it clear that Mexico had her own agenda and remained on equal footing with the United States. As he remarked the next day before boarding his train, in a private conversation with Titcomb: ' "Defeat' is a word I have never learned. It was necessary to await the time when arrangements could be made in such manner that the complete success of the project would be assured. I wish to . . . assure you that henceforth the interests of the Southern Pacific Company and those of the Mexican Government shall run in parallel lines."[49]

Gracious towards the powerful SP in his speech and afterwards, Obregón nevertheless made his point clear. Development was good, but Mexico would not willingly allow the "imposition of a certain kind of civilization" by U.S. interests.

Mexican newspaper accounts of Obregón's speech also differed subtly but substantially from those of U.S. newspapers. Noted one Mexico City newspaper: "At La Quemada Station, President Obregón gave a talk with the object of solemnly renewing the paralyzed works of the Ferrocarril Sud-Pacífico de México line."[50] In Mexican eyes, the SP de Mex had been paralyzed and was being set free by Mexico. This perspective sharply countered the popular U.S. media view that Mexico was paralyzed and would be set free by the railroad. "With capital Mexico can soon become a self-sustaining empire within itself," noted the *Arizona Republican* in a comment typical of U.S. newspapers.[51] By the time of the pre-construction ceremony, Mexico repeatedly asserted its right to sovereignty in the face of U.S. desires to regulate labor, language, and other aspects of life along the line.

Mexico had taken a number of stabilizing steps following the revolution and considered the railroad's completion an important element in creating a lasting post-revolutionary peace. Having the SP finish the construction effort gave Obregón several important opportunities. Critically, it offered him a chance to work cooperatively with a well-established U.S. company whose ties to the U.S. government had been legendary. The SP was also an icon of determination. It had been one-half of the team that completed the transcontinental railroad in the United States, an event that had generated worldwide headlines.

For its part, the company may have been attempting, from its earliest days, to gain a degree of operational freedom by turning to Mexico as a new business frontier. Railroading in the United States was a profitable but increasingly hostile undertaking. U.S. writers exhorted constantly against the country's "railroad problem" (as if there was just one!)—the corruption and avarice of the large railroad companies—in the 1870s and 1880s.[52] As Charles Crocker, one of the Big Four controlling the SP, noted, "You can get any man to be unfriendly with a railroad after it is built."[53]

The Interstate Commerce Commission, in particular, tightened its regulatory fingers around the SP, and the U.S. government attempted to strengthen its control over the company. By the 1880s, Mexico would have seemed like a welcome oasis not just because of potential profits, but because of a lack of Byzantine U.S.–style regulations as well as the absence of the din of loud denunciations and criticisms. Díaz had enthusiastically encouraged the company to build a line southward into Mexico from Guaymas and, finally, Huntington and Harriman had come. But the dawn of the revolution and the depredations upon SP equipment and trackage created a familiar scene for the railroad. Once again, the large U.S. corporation faced a government as an antagonist, as the railroad tried to obtain reparations for damages done. Rather than emphasizing an attempt at railroad conquest in Mexico, the SP had to adopt a defensive stance against a series of legal and financial challenges.

The revolution also played a vital role in shaping the relationship between the SP de Mex and the government. The military phase of the revolution between 1910–1920 sharpened Mexican expressions of sovereignty, but the conflict also set the tone for the relationship over the next thirty years as well. The railroad felt that the government had a responsibility to recompense it for damages suffered during the conflict. The government, though, considered revolutionary damages as acts of God over which it had no control. It thus felt no responsibility for the depredations suffered by the railroad. The issue of recompensation would subsequently loom over the relationship for most of the railroad's remaining life in Mexico as the two sides fought to determine culpability and obligation.

A large part of this question of rights and responsibilities includes the issue of identity. After Carranza had consolidated power late in the fall of 1915, Mexican-owned railroads had different (and specifically superior) rights and status than U.S.–owned railroads in the country and received accordingly different treatment. This Carranzan priority for Mexican railroads contrasted with Porfirian attitudes and actions, which had strongly encouraged and actively supported U.S. railroads, often more so than Mexican lines. Mexico considered the SP de Mex to be of distinctly U.S. extraction and accordingly treated it as a second-class citizen. It refused to actively provide the company with the same form of aid it gave to the national lines in terms of technical assistance, staffing, advice, and management. It also treated the SP de Mex with aloofness, choosing to ignore the company's difficulties with weather and the revolution. Some of this aloofness might have stemmed from deference to the company's perceived size, wealth, and ability, but more likely, the government absorbed and reflected the country's frustration against the United States and its attempts to violate Mexican sovereignty in the bombing of Veracruz, Pershing's Punitive Expedition, and other U.S. military excursions into the country.

Between 1909 and 1923, the SP de Mex considered itself to be unambiguously North American. It had incorporated in New Jersey and had the patriotic exhortations of Huntington, Harriman, and Randolph behind it. Mexico also considered the company a U.S. one. The ceremonies and the press coverage marking resumption of the line's construction only served to reinforce this U.S. identity. But the question of the railroad's identity would become both more tangled and more urgent with time, as the company began construction of the final gap between Tepic and La Quemada.

CHAPTER 4

"Get Out if You Can"

The Salsipuedes Gorge, Taxes, and
Completion of the Line
(1923–1929)

Between 1923 and 1929, the Southern Pacific of Mexico (SP de Mex; Ferrocarril Sud-Pacífico de México) confronted a series of technical, legal, and financial obstacles while simultaneously encountering regional cultural, religious, and ethnic elements that influenced the company's interactions with Mexican leaders. This chapter probes the first set of issues, followed in the next chapter by an assessment of the influence of the second set of factors during the same general time period.

The immense Barranca de Santo Tomás presented the primary obstacle to completion of the final 162 kilometers into Guadalajara. This engineer's nightmare consisted of a series of ravines up to five miles wide and two thousand feet deep in places. As one journalist noted in 1926, "Just as explorers have dreamed of discovering the North Pole, so railway men have dreamed of finding the way across the barrancas . . ."[1] By November 1924, over four thousand men labored at construction work in the barrancas.

Because of their width, eleven gorges required spanning with steel viaducts, the largest being the Salsipuedes ("get out if you can") Gorge, 860 feet high and 240 feet long. In one twenty-six-kilometer section, workmen drilled twenty-six tunnels into and through a variety of ridges. Pack animals and laborers carried construction materials in by climbing steep trails, often through torrential rains. The rock through which workers cut tunnels and routes had a glass-like consistency, often shattering uncontrollably despite attempts at precise blasting by experienced work crews. As a result, cave-ins occurred, which required cleaning and redrilling in order to continue. The effort to bridge the "washboard of razorback ridges and volcanic escarpments" consisted of, remarked one railroad historian, "some of the hardest railroad construction in transportation history."[2]

At points south of Tetitlán, the line passed directly through lava flows with edges that could cut workmen's footwear to shreds; boards had to be laid to permit workmen to even walk in the area.[3] The four thousand laborers accomplished all of the tunnel drilling, and the attendant cuts and fills, using hand tools, pushcarts, and black powder.[4] When completed, the structure spanning the Salsipuedes Gorge became (and remains) the second-highest railway bridge in Mexico and the fifth-highest in Latin America.

Climatic conditions also hindered construction. The barrancas received rainfall of extraordinary density and duration during the four-year effort. Torrential downpours, up to forty centimeters a day for weeks on end during each fall's rainy season, caused mudslides, hindered mule traffic, and sometimes halted construction for six weeks at a time.[5]

But the company faced still other obstacles besides the daunting terrain, difficult construction, and climate. The issue of reparations from the Mexican government to the SP de Mex arose again and again, Medusa-like. The first post-revolutionary rift in the apparent Pan-American harmony between the government and the railroad appeared in late February of 1924. After construction of the final segment between Tepic and La Quemada had already begun, the government announced that the railroad's agreed-upon recompensation of twenty-three million pesos had been reduced based on a new and unexpected "study and adjustment" of the reparations bills presented by the SP de Mex.[6]

At issue was the percentage of interest owed on the indemnity due the railroad. While the Southern Pacific Company (SP) insisted that 6 percent was an appropriate rate of interest, Director of Railways Manuel Cabrera pointed out that, in analogous cases in the United States, the maximum rate was between 4 percent and 5 percent. Cabrera therefore insisted on a 4.5 percent maximum interest rate, which lowered the amount due to the SP de Mex by about $1.5 million U.S.[7]

The SP de Mex also decided to accept a significant drop in the amount of future bond payments promised by the Mexican government on the reparations debt, from nearly $12 million U.S. to $8 million U.S., and finally agreed publicly to this lower amount in mid-1924. A decline in the peso's value in the previous two years played a partial role in the reduction of monies. But the railroad's acceptance of the lesser sum also occurred in part because of several embarrassing mistakes it had made in negotiating the agreements.

First, SP de Mex President Epes Randolph had in 1917 claimed 152,000 pesos in damages to the Los Alamos branch. Because the Carranza government had not responded to the request for reparations, he resubmitted the claim in 1920, the year before his death. However, in submitting the claim a second time, he increased the amount to 862,000 pesos—perhaps inadvertently, or perhaps based on some internal reappraisal of the true amount he believed was owed to the railroad. The error, if it was an error, was not caught until after the 1923 agreement had been signed.

Second, the SP de Mex officials realized that they had placed letters on file with the government, in which railroad administrators had stated that they were not interested in rebuilding the Tonichi and Los Alamos branches and thought their value was low—thus negating the railroad's current claims that it ought to be reimbursed handsomely for revolutionary damages to the two branch lines.[8] Understandably, too, the reparations study by the Mexican government moved slowly; the railroad had submitted fifty-three volumes of reports detailing damages.[9]

As the reparations owed to the railroad slipped to the first of several increasingly lower levels, construction of the final segment meanwhile began in earnest. Work started almost immediately after the March 1923 signing of the agreement and took just over four years—an inordinately long time for a section of track barely a hundred miles long.[10]

During construction of the final Tepic–La Quemada section, workers excavated more than nine thousand linear meters of rock for the tunnels required to pass through ridges in the mountainous barrancas region. The work required a large labor force. Because neither the SP de Mex nor the SP wanted to tie up thousands of their own employees on the project, they subcontracted the work to the Ogden-based Utah Construction Company (UCC) of the United States. The UCC, which won the contract for completion of the line with a bid of just over $6 million U.S., won over two competing firms.[11] One other company also received a contract for a portion of the work: the firm of Twohy Brothers, which constructed the first fifteen kilometers of the line.[12]

Mexican Government Attitudes Towards Construction

As the work progressed, Mexican government technical inspectors took careful note of the company's progress. The inspectors' reports to the Department of Communications and Public Works (SCOP; Secretaría de Comunicaciones y Obras Públicas) included descriptions of the total volume of cubic meters excavated, the total progress in meters each month, and the amount of masonry performed on tunnels. These reports, which inspectors submitted monthly and broke down into one-week divisions, showed a strong concern for the well-being of the laborers—far more than the SP expressed in its corporate correspondence. Unlike the U.S. firm's technical reports, the SCOP reports almost always included detailed commentary on whether or not work was proceeding safely, what accidents had occurred and why, and what was being done to rectify dangerous elements of the construction effort. Noted one typical report: "In the aforementioned cuts, they [engineers of the Ferrocarril Sud-Pacífico de México] have . . . diminished the danger to the workers; in effect, they have used stronger wood to support tunnels in advance and have proceeded to widen the cut, removing material from the upper part, that has a tendency to collapse. It is the hope that, with some luck, the workers are now safe."[13]

Government inspectors addressed the laborers' well-being in a variety of ways. "In hot climates the workers consume large quantities of water, and they are exhausting their supply almost daily," warned Rafael Luna, a technical inspector in the region, urging a sizable increase in the potable water supply for workers.[14]

The team of inspectors also recommended certain courses of action to the SCOP on a variety of other issues. For instance, as the line neared completion, the SP de Mex petitioned the government to allow it to use work trains between Tepic and Ixtlan in the state of Nayarit to immediately begin moving passengers, mail, and cargo along the newly completed segment of line, rather than waiting several months for fancier and more spacious passenger trains currently under construction. The government took the issue under consideration, and Inspector C. Molina opined to the head of SCOP that "the track is already completely finished and offers perfect stability; and at this date there is nothing to fear; in my view, there is no inconvenience in permitting the Southern Pacific to continue the service it has in place; the work trains, on numerous difficult occasions, have already covered the road for many months."[15]

The technical inspectors, as the government's front line for information about the railroad's progress, illustrated time and time again their close scrutiny of the railroad's progress and conditions during construction. These inspectors reported not just on engineering details but on virtually all aspects of the company's operations, down to and including a shortage of toilet paper for passengers on some trains.[16]

Mexican engineers were also not above asking the SP de Mex for its railroad engineering expertise if problems arose that they could not readily solve. At one point, concrete cracked repeatedly in one tunnel, and inspectors puzzled at length over the causes of the fractures. The head of SCOP finally ordered a subordinate to ask the SP de Mex for technical assistance with the problem, the railroad provided help, and work teams quickly repaired the cracks.[17]

SP de Mex Attitudes Towards Construction

Meanwhile, the administrators of the SP de Mex had their own concerns about railroad construction but acted without having an accurate picture of the difficulties—and thus the delays—faced by laborers until late in the construction effort. Above all else, SP de Mex officials focused on the pace of the line's construction between 1923 and 1927.

SP de Mex President Harvey B. Titcomb wrote repeatedly to W. H. Wattis, UCC president, expressing anger and frustration about the speed and quality of the work being done. Apparently prompted by a previous letter from Wattis requesting a raise for 1,500 of his workers in the barrancas due to the difficulty and danger of the terrain, Titcomb registered his dissatisfaction with the UCC's efforts: "The physical results are not commensurate with the promises and forecasts made," Titcomb noted in 1926. "Definite assurance must be given and the work undertaken in a really vigorous and more expert manner."[18]

In other letters he called the work "sorely disappointing." In a telegram to SP executive Paul Shoup, Titcomb commented that the "work of Utah Construction Company in Mexico is done in such a dilatory way and so lacking in either supervision, energy or skill that it is wholly unsatisfactory and we may have to take summary measures to get the line open, which at present rate of progress on their contract could not happen for years to come." But another factor appeared. Titcomb also noted that "I am told . . . that we have to be cautious with them because they are interested in various kinds of business that give the Company a great deal of commercial freight, which is news to me. Will you please have this statement run down as it is important we have accurate information about their shipments."[19]

The UCC was indeed a stockholder in a number of companies that did business with the SP in the United States, including the Sego Milk Company and the Lion Coal Company, both of which shipped their products on SP lines. However, the UCC's involvement in these and other activities beneficial to the SP did not sway SP executives, and on March 6, 1926 the president of the SP, William Sproule, dragged himself into the fray, firing off a letter to Wattis: "Having returned from Mexico, must confess myself amazed at the lack of progress and dilatory methods in the work covered by your contract with Southern Pacific Railroad Company of Mexico. Reports before you of the lack of progress speak for themselves. Promises made us have not been fulfilled. I request your personal attention to the conditions there because they reflect discredit upon your Company."[20]

However, the problem lay not in any "dilatory" attitude by the UCC, but rather in the exceptional difficulty of working in the barrancas and dealing with various uprisings taking place against the government at the time. In retrospect, the complaints of SP de Mex officials about the supposedly dilatory efforts of the UCC proved overly harsh. The lead engineer for the UCC, J. Q. Barlow, sent a letter to Wattis on March 1, 1926, dutifully noting the difficulty of the terrain, unplanned changes in the route, and the steady rock and mudslides that plagued construction during the rainy season. He also noted that SP de Mex officials had taken an inordinate amount of time to decide just where to place at least one of the tunnels.

The disruptive effects of the Cristero Rebellion (1926–1929) also slowed construction, as did other sporadic popular uprisings against the Calles government. Barlow noted: "On certain parts of the Barranca work the Revolution which was in progress for four months had its effect in blocking the line to supplies." Barlow then added that he thought the UCC was entitled to "any additional time they might claim to complete the contract. . . . we are, in my judgement, entitled to at least a year's extension." His estimate was only two weeks off, as the extension was eventually given and the section was completed fifty-four weeks later.

The two companies battled and bickered with each other for the next several months. None of the SP de Mex's executives felt up to what would have been an arduous and lengthy walk or mule ride through very difficult country to do their own inspection of the segment in question. So in the early summer of 1926, the SP de Mex surreptitiously hired an investigator (referred to only as "Mr. Mayo") to make a quiet visit to the area in question and study it firsthand. More than three years had passed since the start of construction, and railroad officials still lacked a fundamental understanding of the obstacles posed by the terrain.

But even this trip did not resolve the construction issues to the satisfaction of Titcomb—described as "a fighting man, eager to make war on the wilderness"[21]—and he finally made an inspection visit himself. On August 3, he rather sheepishly wrote to Sproule that he "now understands the physical difficulties encountered on the line," also noting in the same letter that "the labor situation has improved considerably and at the present we are about 1,000 men short." The line was chronically understaffed with laborers, despite a high rate of pay.

Besides construction concerns, the railroad also expressed an arrogant attitude both about its role as conqueror and about Mexican law. A comment made by L. J. Spence, the director of traffic for the SP system, epitomized the misperceptions held by administrators. In making an inspection tour of the line in late 1923 as construction got underway, Spence noted that "I warned them [Mexican leaders] that if they look forward to development they must frame and interpret their laws for the protection of foreign life and property."[22] Administrators found it difficult to leave behind their own arrogant preconceptions about Mexico as they entered the country to build a new railroad. They would carry these distorted attitudes throughout their tenure in Mexico.

Completion of the Railroad

Labor crews finally completed the railroad on April 15, 1927, at 2:00 p.m. The four-year effort had cost the company $14 million U.S. For the first time since railroad construction had begun in the country ninety years earlier, businesses and passengers could access the country's entire west coast by rail from Mexico City. Prophetically, however, the ceremonies marking actual completion of the line on May 8, 1927, were subdued. Although railroad officials had planned a lavish celebration, complete with speeches by Mexican presidents Alvaro Obregón and Plutarco Elías Calles, marching bands from both countries, and a grand banquet at the Salsipuedes Gorge, SP de Mex officials reduced the ceremony at the last minute to a far simpler affair, after both Calles (who had originally dictated the date of the event) and Obregón canceled abruptly. A carload of troops escorting a passenger train in the state of Jalisco had been massacred by rebels several weeks earlier (whether they were Cristeros or rebels with other political motivations is uncertain), and the Mexican government, worried about further ambushes, decided to call off its large-scale participation in the ceremony.

All involved agreed that luminaries gathered for a celebration would be potential targets. "Persons who do this would probably consider it much more effective to massacre the kind of party proposed to be gathered at Salsipuedes viaduct," noted Sproule in a coded letter shortly after the massacre. "The occasion is not of sufficient importance to have a large number of them risk their lives," concurred SP executive H. W. deForest.[23]

Los Angeles Times publisher Harry Chandler was also invited but later received a telegram from Shoup, remarking that "it looks as though the entire celebration is off . . . owing to the inability of Mexican Government officials to be present which seemed to me a polite suggestion that it ought not to take place at this time."[24] Although the reasons for downplaying the ceremony were not made public in either country, various members of the media remarked on the peculiarly subdued nature of the event. Noted the *San Francisco Chronicle*: "There was no excitement, no blare of trumpets, no official welcome. The departure from here [Guadalajara] of the first train to go from here to the United States on the same route was similarly without ceremony."[25] Even Titcomb begged off from speaking at the event, noting that "my Spanish is a little rusty and the English speaking people who will be present will have had enough of me already."[26]

But despite the cancellation and the small, muted ceremony that replaced the original gala, both government and railroad officials were deeply satisfied that the construction effort had at last been finished. A fourteen-carat spike (cost: $325 U.S.) was driven by Titcomb on the Salsipuedes Bridge, a few remarks were said to a handful of journalists and SP administrators, and the ceremony was done.

By the time Titcomb nailed that final spike, the railroad had already spliced itself into the Mexican railroad system at its southern terminus in Guadalajara. The National Railways of Mexico (NRM; Ferrocarriles Nacionales de México) had signed agreements with the SP de Mex dictating the joint use of passenger facilities in Guadalajara, the dispersal of revenue earned from jointly used freight trains, and the sharing of costs for new joint facilities.[27]

The first train crossed into Guadalajara two days later, on April 17, at 5:50 on a Sunday evening. Titcomb's speech that day spoke volumes about the company's misperceptions of Mexico: "We do not have to go far into history, about 1850, when to a great extent the entire southland of the United States, especially New Mexico, Arizona, and California, was populated to a great extent by people similar to those we find in Mexico." Titcomb glossed over the fact that the United States had taken Mexico by force and that the people in question were Mexican, and not just "similar" to those found in Mexico. Furthermore, he continued, "Mexico is the logical place. We Americans must enter and develop and get the benefit of the great prosperity that will come to the pioneers who go in there."[28] Titcomb naïvely expected profits to rain upon the railroad like manna from heaven. From the Mexican perspective, though, the country had already struck gold: the nation at last had a railroad network that ran from border to border and from sea to sea—the most comprehensive in Latin America.

SP's Post-Construction Administration of the Line

By the end of 1927, the SP de Mex's management team had assumed the basic form it would retain for the rest of its corporate life. The company had a board of directors consisting of fifteen Americans, four of whom were located in Mexico. The executive board for the railroad consisted of another five men, who conducted virtually all of the day-to-day business of the completed line: Sproule, president of the SP until 1928; C. R. Harding; Paul Shoup, an SP vice president; his brother Guy V. Shoup, an attorney who also served as a member of the company's legal counsel; and W. A. Worthington, all of San Francisco (fig. 4.1).[29] About twenty other Americans and Mexicans also served as officials. They acted as general agents in the towns through which the line passed, served as financial administrators and legal counsel in Mexico, and filled miscellaneous functions as officers. Finally, a committee consisting of four Americans living in Mexico City rounded out the administration of the line. The railroad's administrative staff at the end of 1927 amounted to thirty-eight people, located in all four states through which the line ran, as well as in New York, Chicago, and San Francisco. Nearly four hundred Mexican laborers toiling along the line in various capacities made up the rest of the permanent workforce.

Once the jubilation of completing the line wore off, company officials began expressing reservations about doing business in Mexico. The railroad was busy, as the years 1927–1929 brought steady

4.1 Paul Shoup, president, Southern Pacific Company, 1930. Although Shoup was the president of the entire Southern Pacific system, he took close and personal interest in the operations of the SP de Mex line and remained a key decision maker throughout the railroad's history. (Reproduced by permission of the Huntington Library, San Marino, California, Historic Photo Collections, Image # photCL 91[1757])

4.2 Engine attempting to cross a "shoofly"—designed as a temporary rerouting of the line around construction work—across Mocorito River in August 1918. This image is emblematic of the railroad's difficulties in Mexico. (Reproduced by permission of the Huntington Library, San Marino, California, Southern Pacific of Mexico Collection)

increases in traffic and revenue. But sometimes it must have seemed, from the SP de Mex's perspective, as though some divine but malevolent form of intervention had been aimed unerringly at the company. For instance, weather conditions in Mexico proved far different than the railroad was used to in the semi-arid western United States where most of its lines ran (fig. 4.2). Particularly in Sinaloa and Nayarit states, torrential rains annually washed out costly bridge after bridge, and company officials often expressed despair about the line's future. "It is evident in this tropical country with recurring destructive torrents we have problems yet unsolved," noted Sproule to Titcomb in late 1927. "Indeed, this gives rise to the larger question of whether it is likely to be possible to keep the road open upon any basis that will warrant the investments necessary to accomplish it."[30]

But the SP de Mex resisted abandoning its line. It pushed forward after 1927 despite having steadily lost money since the revolution. Officials hoped that now that the line was completed, the firm would realize greater profits and stability in operations. To that end, they felt that managing the company from within Mexico rather than across the border would give them better control over the line's operations. In the summer of 1927, the company relocated its headquarters from the United States to Guadalajara.

Moving Company Headquarters

The move involved a major undertaking for the small company and raises an important question: If the company felt that its future might well be tenuous in Mexico, why would it make the effort to relocate? Railroad administrators stated explicitly that they felt they could not properly supervise operations from Tucson or anywhere else than actually along the line.[31] The company thought it would be strategically well situated in its new home in Guadalajara because it could oversee operations from the busy southern terminus of the line and could more readily communicate with Mexico City railroad officials. But this reasoning begs the question of why the railroad made such a costly move in the face of increasing signs of possible failure.

By moving the railroad into Mexico, officials wished not only to maintain closer daily administration of the line, but also to take advantage of the benefits of Mexican legal status. But the Mexican government never clarified the company's position as Mexican or U.S. The railroad struggled to gain advantages from being recognized as a Mexican corporation in Mexican courts. Yet incongruously, at times its administrators also desired to maintain legal status as a foreign corporation in Mexican eyes for the advantages gained by that status, and because of their pride in the company's U.S. origins. However, for the railroad to have juridical status as Mexican meant to relinquish assistance from the U.S. government. The U.S. consul in Mexico City, Arthur Schoenfeld, noted in 1928:

> I have been informed by Mr. H. B. Titcomb, president of the Company, that it is a Mexican corporation and that its charter contains a so-called Calvo clause under which the Company agrees not to appeal, under any circumstances, to any foreign government for intervention between it and the Mexican government. Mr. Titcomb stated further that he had scrupulously observed this clause and

that any information which he gave me must be understood to have been given at my solicitation and for my information, and not for purposes of representations to the Mexican government.[32]

But despite having agreed to such a clause, the company continued to press the Mexican government in court to clarify its legal identity. Oddly, the railroad moved to Guadalajara from the United States before this issue was resolved. Later, between 1930 and 1934, the SP de Mex kept an administrative file called "Question of Whether the SP de México is a Mexican or U.S. Company." The fact that the railroad moved into Mexico without resolving this issue first indicates the "act now, react later" attitude many of its officials held—an attitude also visible in the company's problems with its labor force just weeks before the move.

To maintain efficient and continuous operations in Mexico after relocating in Guadalajara, the company needed to convince workers that such a move was in their best interest. The SP de Mex had maintained its headquarters in Tucson since its establishment there by Randolph in 1903 while operating as the Sonora Railway. Relocating company operations into Mexico meant moving all U.S. employees willing to resettle, as well as their families—130 people in all—across the border a thousand miles into Mexico. The SP knew that the idea of moving would be difficult for older employees and urged SP de Mex officials to hire younger workers.

Employees' reluctance to relocate generated some conflict within the company. Many personnel balked at the idea of moving down to Guadalajara. "The SPRC of Mexico is somewhat embarrassed in re-taining its employees," noted Titcomb to Paul Shoup on June 2, 1927, "as many of them do not care to go to Guadalajara." Many workers did not want to live in Mexico and transferred to other SP branch offices in San Francisco and Texas, taking better-paying jobs and keeping their seniority. Titcomb and Sproule quickly decided to for-bid employees from keeping their seniority if they transferred, mak-ing relocation less desirable by forcing them to start as new employees in their new positions elsewhere.

Finding themselves in the role of corporate missionaries, admin-istrators considered recruitment of "the younger generation" a vital element in keeping the line active and well staffed. In a suggestion reminiscent of Horace Greeley's exhortation to "go west and grow with the country," SP official Paul Shoup suggested to Titcomb that "if you find it difficult to secure competent and experienced staff, perhaps some of us could help out by canvassing for some of the younger generation who have not taken root elsewhere and would be glad to try Guadalajara and grow up with the country."[33] The echo of nineteenth-century U.S. attitudes about Mexico as a wild land to be colonized by foreign interests could still be heard through such sentiments, as though Mexico were uninhabited and could not properly "grow up" without assistance.

On a warm evening in late July 1927, ninety employees and forty family members left Tucson in a fourteen-car railroad consort, stopping in Empalme to pick up fifty Mexican-based employees and their dependents also moving to Guadalajara as part of the relocation. The Empalme move stemmed from a consolidation and relocation of construction offices formerly in Empalme and Tepic.[34] The relocation, which cost the company $49,473 U.S., included renovation of the company's new corporate headquarters in the former Hotel Cosmopolita in Guadalajara. The State of Jalisco treated the new arrival well, giving a twenty-thousand-square-meter parcel of land to the railroad for construction of new terminal facilities.[35]

Government Vigilance on the Line, 1927–1929

Meanwhile, as the railroad began operations from its new headquarters, the Mexican government maintained its careful management of the operations of the SP de Mex. The government's technical inspectors scattered along the line's 1,800 kilometers continued to report on SP de Mex activities after completion of the line in 1927. Between 1927 and 1929, despite the Cristero Rebellion and national political upheaval in 1928, passenger and freight traffic ran heavily and steadily along the newly completed line, giving inspectors much to report on. This vigilance focused on three particular topics: the comfort of passengers; safety along the line; and the railroad's general operational efficiency.[36]

Field inspectors emphasized concern for passenger comfort and welfare. "I note that passengers are often standing rather than being provided with seats, leading to public protests," one inspector remarked shortly after the line began operations between Nogales and Guadalajara. He also pointed out the need for heating in the lesser classes of passenger service.[37] Passenger comfort issues arose frequently from the Mexican perspective but rarely from the administrators of the SP de Mex. Remarked Inspector Alberto Crespo in 1929, "The flow of passengers on the line is causing a very bad impression, and confusion." Apparently the number of passengers crammed into two Pullman sleepers, two first-class cars, and three second-class cars, hitched together in a long consort with an additional three mail cars and "four or five" cargo cars per trip, was creating "a very disagreeable public spectacle." The inspector recommended the addition of several third-class cars and suggested that the government offer its own service from Nogales to Guaymas to help relieve the line's heavy thrice-weekly traffic load.[38]

Sometimes passenger problems stemmed from the railroad's successes. Profits in 1928 and 1929 reached 378,000 pesos and 452,000 pesos respectively, after the company suffered losses of more than a million dollars in 1927.[39] SP de Mex officials had no particular problems with the full cars and crowded passenger terminals that came with heavy use of the line by shippers and passengers; these qualities signified prosperity for the company (fig. 4.3). But Mexican inspectors pointed out the need to correct inefficiencies of the SP de Mex station at Nogales, where the customs office stayed open for only two hours during each of the three days of service, forcing passengers to rush into the ticket office just before departure. One inspector offered sensible suggestions: "Make the company sell tickets both the day before and after departure," he reasoned, "and keep the customs office open for far more hours." The inspector emphasized the passengers' rights: "We must give them all the room and facilities they deserve," he concluded.[40] Inspectors also noted other issues of comfort and safety such as poor water service for passengers on Pullman coaches; the occasional episode of vandalism along the line; and schedule changes.

The second area of concern—the safety of SP de Mex operations—

4.3 Vendors at a stop selling food to SP de Mex passengers. (Courtesy of Donald Duke, Golden West Books, San Marino, California)

also fell under the watchful eye of SCOP inspectors. Because SCOP had responsibility for all of Mexico's transportation issues, it had the authority to order a wider range of changes than if it had been solely responsible for railroads. If SCOP inspectors found poorly marked train crossings or noted unsafe truck ramps leading from the railroad's right-of-way, inspectors politely and concisely informed the railroad of these deficiencies.[41] If sewer lines or telegraph facilities posed potential hazards, inspectors quickly noted those as well.[42]

Other examples abound of the government's desire to maintain high standards of safety in maintenance and engineering. The interim subsecretary of SCOP remarked in a note to Earl B. Sloan, the indefatigable young chief engineer of the SP de Mex, that the reconstruction of bridges at several points along the line had not been done with proper safety in mind.[43] Without protest, company engineers redid the work.

Several examples also exist of the Mexican government's control over a third area: that of the company's efficiency in operations. The government dictated what types of rolling stock should run along the tracks. Unhappy with the ratio of passenger trains to produce trains and desirous of increased passenger service, one senior SCOP official suggested to the railroad that it provide more of the passenger trains and fewer of the vegetable cars.[44] Although the SP de Mex made far more money off the shipment of winter vegetables than on passenger traffic, it complied with the inspector's recommendations without apparent dissent. The government also carefully watched the railroad's schedules, occasionally asking it to correct chronically late trains and to make connections with NRM lines in a more timely fashion.

Continuing Troubles with the 10 Percent Tax and Reparations

Meanwhile, as Mexican officials watched and administered these three aspects of the SP de Mex's operations—passenger safety, passenger comfort, and general operational efficiency—a series of legal problems dogged the company. The most troublesome of these was the issue of the 10 percent tax. The railroad owed this amount to the government. But the government in turn owed money to the railroad for reparations. Because the Cristeros, the Yaquis, and other combative factions in the country regularly damaged SP de Mex properties, the company kept submitting claims for these damages, holding the Mexican government liable as it had done between 1910 and 1920.[45]

The Mexican government's 10 percent tax on the railroad's gross revenue involved more than the government simply taxing the railroad's income, because the government also used the tax as a bargaining chip to defray a variety of expenses, including, but not limited to, the reparations owed. For instance, every time the SP de Mex claimed a debt of some kind against Mexico, the government would allow the railroad to retain the 10 percent tax but would apply that amount against notes or other debts owed by the government. In doing so, the government fell further and further behind on its debt to the railroad because the amounts claimed by the railroad often totaled more than 10 percent of its gross revenue each year.

The railroad and the government had been negotiating almost continually over the issue of the 10 percent tax since it had been passed in early 1923. In 1929, the railroad submitted claims to the government of 1.5 million pesos, dealing mainly with depredations caused by rebels between 1928 and 1929.[46] The claims commission reduced the amount to 900,000 pesos. The railroad refused the payment, holding out hopefully for the entire sum.

The Calles government successfully pleaded poverty as its rationale for its inability to pay for current bills for depredations as well as older debts dating back to the revolution. Because the railroad could not audit the government's books, while the government could closely inspect the railroad, company officials were forced to take the government at its word on Mexico's precise financial status.

Simply put, the government owed the railroad money and had owed it money for a long time. Mexican officials had good reasons for the delays. Government coffers were low on cash and Calles's spending priorities lay elsewhere, particularly as the Cristero Rebellion grew and required an increasingly larger outlay in troops and supplies. The government commission assigned to study the problem had many tens of thousands of pages of evidence to sort through, and the SP's claims contained inconsistencies in dollar amounts owed.

Railroad officials became frustrated with the protracted wait for payment, and expressions of corporate desire to actually take steps to get rid of the line began to surface as early as 1928, even as the company turned unprecedented profits. The unknown ability of the government to pay the reparations monies in the future greatly discouraged railroad officials. "Some personal and direct discussion of what the Mexican policy towards this railroad will be and our readiness to turn it over to Government at cost is most probably all upon which we have to sound them out at first," noted Sproule in January 1928, writing to SP Vice President Angus D. McDonald. Sproule also showed the same preoccupation with issues of time and chronology that had dogged the company during construction: "These negotiations may be protracted owing to procrastination of the Mexican mind and difficulties natural to such a negotiation under the circumstances," he warned in the same letter.[47]

Another related factor also appeared in 1928: the U.S. government's own reticence to confront Mexico over financial matters. Sproule cabled SP official H. W. deForest in New York that, following a conference to discuss Mexican finances and the American Bankers Committee, "those present at the Mexico City conference referred to (Ambassador [Morrow] wishes not to be quoted) believe far better for the bankers to allow the Mexican government to meet its domestic obligations and so help towards improving confidence of investors at this time."[48]

The railroad subsequently lessened its insistence on securing reparations from the Mexican government and at the same time appeared more resigned to continuing payment of the 10 percent tax. U.S. Ambassador to Mexico Dwight Morrow figured prominently into the Mexican–SP equation, and brought tidings to the railroad that further weakened its resolve to push Mexico City for repayment of debts it felt the government legally owed it:

> I have had long talks with Mr. Montes de Oca [Mexico's secretary of state and of the Department of Finance and Public Credit] and both days brought up the subject of his payments to you. I regret to say that the information which he gave me was not very encouraging . . . He is still, so far as cash is concerned, in the situation of never having much more than enough on hand to meet his bimonthly payrolls. . . . Of course, he is under just as great an obligation to pay you for your transportation services as he was to pay the U.S. Government for the rifles he bought from them and various manufacturers and supply houses for airplanes and other war supplies . . .[49]

But despite this information about the difficult financial straits of the Mexican government and the corresponding unlikeliness of receiving payments anytime soon, railroad executives continued to express warm but vague hopes for future successes in Mexico, relying wishfully on sentiments of support from the U.S. government. "The problems the Mexican government have [sic] are keeping the peace, adjusting the national debt on a basis which will permit promises to be kept, disposing of the Church controversy, and putting the agrarian land settlement on a more businesslike basis," explained Paul Shoup to SP President Hale Holden. He continued hopefully:

> Mr. Morrow is a great asset in this situation. He has the full confidence of the Mexican Government ... he is following what seems to me to be the most sensible policy of having the Government put its house in order and meeting its current obligations as it goes. There are some of the foreign element in Mexico, especially those to whom the Government owes money, who do not approve of this policy, and who feel that the United States by wielding a big stick could do much more than is being done to make Mexico keep the peace and pay all its debts. From all I could learn while in Mexico, it seems to me Mr. Morrow's course is infinitely the better one.[50]

Although SP de Mex officials talked ambitiously and arrogantly at times, they had never aggressively confronted Mexico. Morrow's desire for consensus rather than conflict rendered them even less willing to push the Mexican government over monetary issues. However, the other "foreign elements"—in particular, U.S. companies in Mexico— met with much more consistent financial and operational success in Mexico. Based on SP de Mex reactions to the Nicaraguan situation and the Mexican Revolution, the Mexican government knew the SP de Mex would be unlikely to agitate for U.S. intervention in the country. But Mexican relations with other types of U.S. business interests varied markedly.

Many other businesses had come to the country after the revolution. U.S. mining and manufacturing sectors consistently performed well economically after 1920, unlike the SP de Mex.[51] Mexico also did not regulate other U.S. businesses as successfully as it did the SP de Mex. The numerous U.S. oil companies doing business in Mexico at the same time as the SP de Mex, for instance, enjoyed greater latitude. The nation needed to make its petroleum available for foreign exploitation to give the country access to foreign loans for rebuilding the war-torn country and to boost the legitimacy of its post-revolutionary governments.[52] Twenty-six oil companies operated in Mexico at the

end of the revolution. "Under the circumstances, the domestic authorities did not ignore the foundation of a most American-like industry in
Mexico, but they could do little about it," notes one historian.[53]

Mexico's desire to placate U.S. political and corporate interests
over the issue of petroleum made Mexican leaders far more disposed
to enter into discussions with corporations and the U.S. government
over issues of reparations in particular than it was with the SP de Mex.
Mexican oil companies also agitated much more readily with Mexico
than did the SP de Mex. "The big U.S. oil operators were the most
adamant of any group of Americans dealing regularly with Mexico in
their refusal to accommodate the postrevolutionary government,"
notes Linda Hall.[54]

The obstacles of geography, misconceptions of conquest, and the
hard reality of law strongly influenced the railroad's course during the
seven years from 1923 to 1929. The SP re-entered Mexico as proud
adventurers when it first began resumption of the line in 1923. Press
accounts glorified the difficulties and drama of the struggle and exhorted the railroad to push through the barrancas. Railroad officials'
preoccupation with advancing the line through the difficult terrain in
a timely fashion outweighed any thoughts of abandoning the effort.
Much like the French in Panama in the last quarter of the nineteenth
century, where any reasonable group might have given up or passed
the effort to another company, the SP pushed on, even though construction took considerably longer than expected and cost the railroad $12 million U.S. and four years to bridge a 103-mile gap.

But the railroad forged ahead between 1923 and 1927, exhorted by
the U.S. press to realize the dreams of Edward H. Harriman, the
railroad magnate who had headed the SP after Collis P. Huntington's
death at the end of the century, and of Randolph, the SP de Mex's first
president. "Randolph's Great Dream Comes True," "E. H. Harriman's
Dream of Railway Development," "Dream of E. H. Harriman Nears
Realization," "One of Harriman's Dreams a Reality in Mexico," and
"Rail Dream of Epes Randolph Unites Mexico" read various headlines
and news items between 1922 and 1927.[55] The work served as a point of
pride for the railroad, a sentiment that may have contributed to its
costly push to finish the line, despite increasingly strong signals from

inside and outside the company that forecasting its income or expenses would prove very difficult or perhaps even impossible because of the unpredictability of future Mexican debt payments or the 10 percent tax.

Mexico's past erratic reparations payments to the railroad, along with the government's extraction of the 10 percent tax, caused the company considerable frustration. Government leaders used law as a regulatory mechanism not just by taxing the railroad, but also by refusing to pay because of bankruptcy and then forcing the railroad to enter into very lengthy litigation for possible—but not certain—remuneration. Hoping to coax Mexico into some kind of cooperation and political stability, the U.S. government was unwilling to rock Mexico's financial boat by supporting the SP de Mex in its battles to extract monies from the Mexican government.

The parent company's size and reputation also worked against its subsidiary and in Mexico's favor. In 1927, the SP was the second-largest company in the United States, with over $2.2 billion U.S. in assets. The company had 58,000 stockholders, 96,000 employees, and 13,532 miles of line covering North America. It also continued to turn profits, having paid a 6 percent dividend to stockholders since 1906.[56] To Mexican leaders, financial backing of this magnitude would have meant that Mexico could be less concerned about causing any possible negative effect, and more concerned with its own agendas of efficiency, safety, and adherence to Mexican railroad law. This appropriate emphasis on Mexican goals and needs was a far cry from the mid-Porfirian era, when President Porfirio Díaz made concessions to foreign railroad companies without appearing to weigh the ill effects on Mexican workers or upon the handful of Mexican-owned railroad companies struggling for survival in the face of foreign railroad investment.

Technical, financial, and logistical aspects of Mexican and U.S. management of the line comprised important components of the relationship between the government and the railroad during the critical years of 1923–1929. However, another very different set of elements simultaneously influenced governmental attitudes and railroad operations during these years: the roles of ethnicity, religion, and race along the Mexican west coast.

CHAPTER 5

Multicultural Mosaic

The Impacts of Otherness
(1923–1929)

Two currents of "otherness" swirled around the Southern Pacific of Mexico (SP de Mex; Ferrocarril Sud-Pacífico de México) during this period. The first consisted of the effects on the line of various real or perceived ethnic, cultural, and religious conflicts—specifically, the role of the Chinese and the Yaqui Indians in Sonora; the threat of dangers posed by Mormon workers; and the actions of the Cristeros along the southern end of the line. The Chinese served as laborers on the line, and the Yaquis both worked on the line and agitated against it at different times. The Mormons served as laborers along the line by the thousands. The Cristero rebels also acted as both workers and rebels, alternately assisting and obstructing the railroad's progress.

The second aspect of otherness at work consisted of Mexican attitudes about the "otherness" of the railroad itself—how groups viewed the railroad as foreign to Mexico, and how the railroad itself contributed to its isolation by emphasizing its differences from, rather than its ties to, Mexican life. In particular, the joint Mexican/American community built by the SP de Mex in Empalme serves as an example of the ways that the railroad's U.S. workers accentuated their differences from its Mexican employees.

Sonora's isolation from central Mexico further inflated the importance of these conflicts, accentuating the differences of the aforementioned groups as well as magnifying the railroad's own foreign identity. Blocked from central Mexico by the Sierra Madre Occidental and more than a thousand miles north of Guadalajara, Sonora remained a region apart in a number of ways. The area had a far less homogeneous racial makeup than central Mexico. The mobile immigrants were highly disparate in appearance, dress, and cultural norms. A frontier mentality of seeking new opportunities shaped their approach to life in the region.[1] Some, such as the Chinese and the Mormons, had actually been invited to settle in the region early in the Porfiriato. But many of these groups faced opposition from both the central government and regional forces within Sonora between 1923 and 1929—and the railroad served as a focal point for these conflicts.

The Anti-Chino League of Sonora and the Railroad

Mexico did not experience the same wave of European immigration as had Argentina and Brazil in the nineteenth century. However, other foreign immigrant groups played significant roles in Mexico. During the Porfiriato, Mexican leaders encouraged Chinese to immigrate following innumerable failed attempts to colonize less-populated regions with Europeans.

"Europeans would not accept the lifestyle of the Mexican laborer," remarked Development Minister Vicente Riva Palacio in 1877 in a report to the Mexican Congress. "European immigrants wished to settle near population centers, where they were not needed." He later noted that "it seems to me that the only colonists who could establish themselves or work on our coasts are Asians . . . This is not an idle dream."[2] Mexico pursued an aggressive colonization policy with China from 1884 until 1900, and by the end of President Porfirio Díaz' rule more than thirteen thousand Chinese resided in Mexico. In Latin America, only Cuba had a larger Chinese population.

Chinese laborers often took railroad jobs on foreign-owned lines because of the high rate of pay, which allowed them to return money overseas to China relatively quickly. They worked in large numbers on the Tehuantepec Railroad, on the Mexican Central Railroad (MCR; Ferrocarril Central Mexicano), and on the SP de Mex. They also began working as entrepreneurs in Sonora and throughout the northwest of the country and quickly came to dominate shoe and clothing manufacturing, owning some of the largest mercantile establishments in Sonora.[3]

But Mexican distrust and dislike of the Chinese residents of the country also existed and had manifested itself since the start of the Porfiriato. Although they constituted a small percentage of the country's population, the Asians stood out. They had different phenotypes and habits, often did not speak Spanish, provided economic competition in some types of business, and were easily identified as "other" and thus "non-Mexican." Chinese immigrants also frequently carried a number of supposedly infectious diseases, including trachoma (a contagious disease of the eye) and beriberi (a disease of the nervous system caused by thiamin deficiency and often mistakenly considered contagious). Late in the Porfiriato, government leaders began to discriminate regularly against the Chinese, noting their anti-national character: "It is not in the national interest to permit the continued unrestricted development of Chinese immigration in a collective form," noted the minister of the interior in 1903.[4]

These attitudes set the stage for revolutionary and post-revolutionary perceptions of the Chinese. To many Mexicans, the Chinese simply corrupted Mexico by their presence in the land. As Alan Knight has noted: "Damned if they miscegenated, the Chinese were damned if they didn't; their separateness—'otherness'—gave rise to bizarre speculations and fantasies."[5]

The most prominent anti-Chinese force in northwestern Mexico after the revolution was the Anti-Chino League of Sonora. The league's slogan was "Por La Patria y Por La Raza," and it consisted of Sonoran businessmen and government leaders who felt they had the nation's best interests at heart. The Anti-Chino League found the presence of the Chinese in the state to be intolerable.

The Chinese, who had immigrated as both entrepreneurs and as laborers, had a variety of interactions with the SP de Mex in Sonora. They had a long history of experience with railroad labor in the hemisphere and had played a critical labor role in the completion of the U.S.'s transcontinental railroad. In Mexico, companies had used them as laborers on a variety of National Railways of Mexico (NRM; Ferrocarriles Nacionales de México) projects. But of the thirty U.S. railroad concerns operating under the NRM, not one ran in Sonora, and the SP de Mex was the only railroad in the state with which they could find employment.[6]

Writing several times in 1930 to the Department of Communications and Public Works (SCOP; Secretaría de Comunicaciones y Obras Públicas), Carlos Tijerina, the league's president, complained at length about the "prevailing and unheard-of immorality" of using Asian workers to build a new station for the SP de Mex at the border in Nogales. The railroad company had used Chinese as well as Japanese as laborers when the Sonora Railway was constructed in the 1880s and had continued to employ them during and after the revolution for maintenance, repairs, and building of new structures.[7]

Tijerina worried about these Chinese labor elements working on the new station and asked the director of SCOP to stop construction of the building or to at least place the project more squarely under federal control. In the process, Tijerina appealed to the SCOP's "well-seated patriotic love" because the project was of "national interest." The secretary of the Anti-Chino League also unabashedly offered an out-of-sight, out-of-mind, "not-in-my-backyard" solution "asking that this project be carried out elsewhere in order to satisfy the Railway's interest, without damaging ours." The SCOP responded almost immediately, remarking that although the SP de Mex had not submitted a plan for any new station, they would "certainly keep the Anti-Chino League's concerns in mind."[8]

The Anti-Chino League also wanted to make clear its place in the lawful scheme of things. With perhaps a touch of overprotestation, they proclaimed their legitimacy: "We stick together as good compatriots, and what we long for is completely lawful and possible, as we are entirely legal and right in using all the means in our possession to triumph. We have constancy. We are not dismayed. Our ranks are swelling. Our works towards utopia move us all forward by patriotism. . . ."[9]

For the Anti-Chino League, "utopia" consisted of a country where the Chinese might be allowed to stay but had virtually no rights. For example, the league proposed that Chinese men not be allowed to marry Mexican women or take certain jobs, including work on the railroad. The league did desire people in the region who would be capable of "forming a more united people [pueblo], more homogeneous . . ." The league specifically wanted to omit any groups from outside the country that were "greatly distant ethnically and linguistically, and which have other social characteristics with respect to ours."[10] Although the league claimed to want to exclude any group that differed radically from the normal Mexican (whatever that might constitute), and thus professed to be acting democratically in whom it chose to exclude, it did not point specifically by name to any other undesirable group besides the Chinese.

However, despite such wishes to exclude the Chinese, many organizations needed them for labor. They worked rapidly, efficiently, and cheaply and flowed into Mexico in a steady stream during the 1923–1929 period, partly driven out of the United States by anti-Chinese sentiments there. Some served as laborers on the SP de Mex's final construction push through the barrancas. The SP de Mex also carried Chinese immigrants into Mexico from the port cities of Nogales, Guaymas, and Mazatlán, and from those points to Tepic to serve as laborers. But wherever they went in the country, the Chinese were feared or disliked, even while at the same time many needed them as laborers. It was a tension that was not—and still has not been—easily reconciled.

The Yaquis and the Railroad

The railroad also used Yaquis as laborers. But, unlike the Chinese, the natives fought back vigorously against attempts to violate their rights, doing battle against what they considered as increasing encroachments on their communal lands. The Yaquis had regular, if often contentious, ties with the SP de Mex. The native group had traditionally occupied a large area of well-irrigated land along the lower Yaqui River, a potentially rich agricultural area in Sonora, since precolonial times. But industrialization and economic growth led to disruption of the Yaquis, as foreign and Mexican interests pushed onto their lands.

To Díaz and other leaders, the Yaquis had blunted Porfirian notions of progress. In the late Porfiriato, the Mexican leader deported thousands of Yaquis to the Yucatán Peninsula to work as henequen laborers, describing them as "antiprogressive elements."[11] The natives viewed both the government and the railroad as usurpers who used force to take their communal landholdings. Because the railroad passed directly through this region, the Yaquis and the SP de Mex clashed primarily over issues of land use and ownership. (Sometimes the conflict became highly personal. In June 1908 Manuel de la Hoz, the legal counsel for the Sonora Railway, was attacked by two Yaquis while he was riding on horseback on a hunting trip. They fired upon each other, with de la Hoz killing one Yaqui and chasing the other away.)[12]

But while some Yaquis fought as rebels, another faction consisted of laborers. Parallel with the clashes of the Yaquis with railroad and government leaders over the decades, Yaqui labor played a significant role in the line's completion. Thousands of them had lived along the SP de Mex's right-of-way for many years as squatters, and the railroad tolerated them as such because of their usefulness as laborers to the company.[13] By 1923, the Yaquis had reached a tenuous peace with both state and railroad and worked as laborers alongside other Mexicans, Chinese immigrants, and Mormons from Utah on the final leg of the railroad. But because the relationship between the government and the Yaquis could dissolve into violent conflict at any time, their work on the railroad as laborers often proceeded in fits and starts, contributing to construction delays.

Barley Yost, the United States's Guaymas consul, noted shortly after construction of the final leg had begun that Yaqui laborers were unhappy with ongoing discussions of land ownership. A work stoppage led to a conference on the controversy. After protracted discussions, the government and the Yaquis reached a satisfactory agreement. Yost noted that after the conference, led by then–Secretary of Finance Adolfo de la Huerta, the latter having good relations with the Yaqui leaders, "the Yaquis withdrew their protest. It is rumored here that a considerable sum of money was promised the Yaquis as a condition of their withdrawal. The railroad company was not a party to the controversy. A large number of Yaqui workmen are employed on the road, it being hoped that this will help to appease them. They are considered good laborers."[14]

However, the peace was short-lived, and within a few months the Yaquis were skirmishing again, launching guerrilla raids on properties throughout northern Mexico and targeting the SP de Mex line as one of the objects of their disaffections.

Yaqui depredations caused 250,000 pesos in damages to the line between September 12 and October 8, 1923, and worried SP de Mex administrators. President Harvey B. Titcomb authorized a bonus to help deal with the "unrest and slight fear" manifested by workers completing the line; the bonus was to be good for four subsequent months and paid to all engineers, transitmen, instrumentmen, and masonry inspectors. Furthermore, men who had been robbed in isolated camps along the line would be reimbursed for their clothing and money.[15] The company also purchased a radio, rented a home, and set up a community boarding house for the single men at Tepic, a move "absolutely essential to hold our men and provide some amusement" in the face of "rather unbearable" living conditions and fears about the Yaquis.

Mexican President Plutarco Elías Calles expressed particular venom towards the Yaquis. As a general during the revolution, he had ordered and directed the savage military campaign against the Yaquis during Venustiano Carranza's rule.[16] Calles maintained an antagonistic stance towards the natives throughout his presidency. As a property owner in Sonora, he may have been worried about the effects of Yaqui agitations on the value of his holdings, which were located near the Yaqui Valley.

Mexican military leaders had difficulty controlling the Yaquis in their homelands in Sonora for several reasons. The natives had great mobility and remained well informed of officials' travel plans, as evidenced by one of the final Yaqui attacks in the late summer of 1926. Former president Alvaro Obregón, who had been busy developing land parcels for sale in the Yaqui Valley, was en route on an SP de Mex train to the border, just south of Guaymas, along with SP de Mex General Manager J. A. Small, when his train was ambushed by Yaquis. The Yaquis apparently believed that Mexican authorities in Hermosillo were holding a tribal commission captive and wanted an audience with Obregón to discuss the situation. The Yaquis held the passengers and crew hostage for five days, as two firing lines of heavily armed Yaquis guarded the train. Federal troops eventually arrived, fierce fighting ensued, and the government acted swiftly and brutally. Over twenty thousand Mexican troops, aided by aerial bombardment, were brought in to put an end to the Yaqui uprisings, this time for good. The conflict put SP de Mex trains out of commission through Yaqui territory for more than a month.[17]

Sometimes Yaqui depredations led to inter-ethnic clashes. For instance, the Yaqui invaded a Guaymas hacienda populated primarily with Japanese. (Sonora had 398 Japanese residents out of the state's 360,000 total by 1930.)[18] The Japanese fought off the Yaqui attack and then requested permission from the Mexican government to fight against the Yaquis in more formal fashion. "It is stated that the request will be granted," noted one newspaper article.[19]

The Mexican press, particularly in central Mexico, often echoed the anti-Yaqui sentiments held by the government and the railroad. Mexico City papers in particular described the Yaquis as lawless marauders. "Troops in Pursuit of Outlaw Band Which Had Committed Many Murders Previous to Latest Outrage," noted a typical headline.[20]

Newspapers in northern Mexico considered the SP de Mex's expansion farther south into the country as a crucial factor in the irregular Yaqui pacifications. They also had more benign attitudes towards the Yaquis than did their Mexico City counterparts: "Undoubtedly, the building of the . . . railroad is the principal factor in bringing about peace as it is the thing above all others which will build up the rich state of Sonora and the Pacific Coast . . . The Yaquis are generally acknowledged to be the best native workers in all Mexico. They are needed badly in Sonora. If peace can be made they will be a valuable asset in the future progress of that state."[21]

Of all the ethnically and racially diverse groups with ties to the railroad during this period, the Yaquis faced the lengthiest and fiercest attacks from the government. They had resided in the country for much longer than the Chinese or the Mormons. Yet with powerful claims to the land, they resisted assimilation into Mexican mainstream culture more strongly than any of the other groups, preferring to risk extinction as a group rather than surrender.

Mormon Workers and the SP de Mex

Mormons from the United States began entering Mexico in significant numbers in 1875, when Mormon founder Brigham Young sent groups of missionaries into the country to proselytize. They soon found that ample room existed for settlements, and in 1880, Díaz gave permission to the Mormons to begin a permanent colony in the state of Chihuahua. The missionaries named this settlement "Colonía Díaz" and quickly established a series of other settlements in the Sierra Madre Occidental.[22]

They had initially come to convert Mexicans to the Mormon religion, but their primary motivation to be in Mexico soon changed. In 1884, the U.S. Supreme Court upheld federal laws making the practice of polygamy a crime, and Mormons in the United States felt the increasing pressure of prejudice from their own government. They began moving into Mexico primarily to seek refuge from persecution in their own country and to freely practice their religious beliefs. In the process, the Mormons added a new element of religion to a country already conscious of the great weight of the Catholic faith. The Mormons lived quietly in the Mexican northwest throughout the Porfiriato. By the end of Díaz' rule, they had established eight profitable colonies in the state of Chihuahua.

Government concerns over the Mormons' religious differences first surfaced in the context of the railroad in 1923. Thousands of Mormon laborers from Utah worked for the Utah Construction Company (UCC), which had just been hired to begin construction work through the barrancas, and government leaders expressed concerns over their upcoming presence in the country. Officials in Obregón's administration commented on the possible moral and religious influence of the several thousand Mormon railroad workers from Utah. One expression of government anxiety appears in a letter from the Mexican consul in Salt Lake City: "All of the chiefs and employees which belong to the [Utah Construction] company are Mormons and clearly associated with this church," remarked Consul J. E. Anchondo, writing to Amado Aguirre, the secretary of foreign relations, on May 28, 1923:

The church's type of work will allow them to get to know and appreciate the enormous natural resources of our west coast, and they would also realize how easy it would be for their missionaries to promulgate their theories among the populations of such region, people who, unfortunately, continue to be under the Spanish yoke. . . . I repeat that the Mormons are going to propagate their doctrine to such population and I believe that this occurrence would pose some danger if it influences the people into believing in it. These *paisanos*, wanting to find a way to rid themselves of the Spaniards who financially control Nayarit, would see the Mormons as some sort of saviors. Since I know this region well, as well as its inhabitants, and also knowing the Mormons' capability in this Capital, it would not be too adventuresome to say that they would do whatever it takes to conquer our people, and if unfortunately they achieve this goal, we would need another Juárez in order to be able to separate the church's own interests in exploiting and victimizing the people wherever they go.[23]

The undersecretary of foreign relations, Eduardo Ortíz, answered the letter on Aguirre's behalf. "We estimate that the Mormons' propaganda will naturally be undercut during their stay in the coastal region. In any case, given the terms established in Constitutional Article No. 130, we are capable of impeding, if necessary, illegal activities of the Mormon priests."[24] Perhaps government faith in the constitution's efficacy made the issue moot in its eyes. Article 130 specifically gave federal authorities the power to "exercise in matters of religious worship and outward ecclesiastical forms such intervention as by law authorized."[25] The government wanted to control the railroad's use of Mormons as laborers because of potential religious differences and appeared ready to use legal mechanisms as necessary to control the SP de Mex's subcontractor, the UCC, to do so.

The differences in degrees of religious tolerance found in 1923, and later in 1926 when the Cristero Rebellion broke out and seriously affected SP de Mex operations, stemmed largely from differences in the attitudes of Obregón and Calles. Both men insisted they were not anti-religion, but simply did not want priests and clergymen agitating the masses over religious issues. But while Calles expressed impatience, Obregón viewed solutions to religious conflict as long-term and evolutionary.[26] The issue was primarily one of tolerance, and Obregón exhibited considerably more patience, or at least diplomacy, in matters of religion. Thus, the Mormon presence in 1923, although significant enough to elicit comment, caused little distress to the political elite in Mexico City. But the government began to react with new vigor against religious freedom of expression in 1926, and the Cristero Rebellion erupted.

The Cristero Rebellion and the SP de Mex, 1926–1929

If Obregón served as the mostly loving midwife responsible for breathing new life into the SP de Mex and overseeing the agreement between government and railroad to complete the line, then Calles (1924–1928) acted as the stern foster parent of the young railroad. The taciturn Sonoran-born Calles exhibited classical nineteenth-century liberal tendencies and responded to events in Mexico based on his antagonistic attitudes towards the Catholic Church. Less eager to embrace U.S. corporations than his predecessor and less interested in cloaking antagonism towards the railroad in the guise of consensus, Calles stimulated a number of national and international events that had direct consequences for the SP de Mex.

Calles's anti-clericalism had never been a secret. When he took office in December 1924, he promptly appointed strategic cabinet members who sympathized with his views on the need for sharp delineation between church and state. The 1917 Mexican Constitution had given the state the right to control the clerical profession, although both Carranza and Obregón had carefully steered clear of exercising that right. However, Calles passed legislation in 1926 that made infringements in civil matters by religious leaders criminal offenses. Hundreds of bishops responded by suspending church services on July 31, 1926, and the conflict became violent and widespread.

The Cristeros rose up in protest against the Calles government and the restrictions it had imposed on the clergy. Located at the tail end of the railroad's territory as well as points farther south, the bulk of the Cristeros came from the states of Michoacán, Jalisco, Guanajuato, and Nayarit—largely rural areas populated by people whose lives had been deeply permeated with Catholic ritual and worship. While certainly not exclusively aimed at the SP de Mex, Cristero depredations caused very heavy damages to the railroad, especially in Nayarit and Jalisco, and severely limited the railroad's ability to function along many portions of its newly completed line.

Between July 1927 and March 1928, the Cristero ranks nearly doubled in size, growing from twenty thousand to thirty-five thousand men actively engaged in fighting against the central government. By the end of the conflict in 1929, fully fifty thousand Cristeros had taken up arms.[27] Because of its nature, the fighting took place in largely non-urban settings far from Mexico City—areas through which many hundreds of kilometers of SP de Mex trackage ran. The Cristeros were rarely far from a section of SP de Mex track.

On December 23, 1927, three hundred rebels burned one of the railroad's largest structures—a seven-hundred-foot railroad bridge thirty kilometers north of Tepic, in the state of Nayarit, the geographic heart of "Cristero country." The SP de Mex estimated that repairs would take up to six weeks to complete, rendering through traffic to Guadalajara and Mexico City impossible because there was no easy way to quickly build a new bridge. However, the lucrative tomato season was in full swing, and the company made provisions to reroute the tomatoes up the coast by boat and thence across the San Blas River in Sinaloa.

Rebel skirmishes against the line continued in the form of smaller marauding bands, and on January 3, 1928, the railroad announced the indefinite suspension of all train service south of Mazatlán. The degree of organization of the Cristeros in Jalisco and Nayarit states "thoroughly embarrassed" the Mexican government by managing to completely stop railroad communication between Guadalajara and Mazatlán.[28] Rebels dynamited and destroyed bridges in La Quemada; tore up track in various locations along the line; attacked trains near the station of El Guamíchil, north of Mazatlán; brought down bridges north of Culiacán; and undertook a number of other traffic-stopping actions.

The conflict proved a very costly one for the railroad, in its estimation even more expensive than the Mexican Revolution. "The last report from Mr. Titcomb . . . indicates the damage to our property may exceed that of any previous revolution," warned A. D. MacDonald of the Southern Pacific Company (SP) to fellow SP executive Hale Holden on March 19, 1929. Titcomb's estimate of damages suffered by the railroad up to that point from Cristero depredations totaled $404,000 U.S.[29]

The railroad also sparred with its parent company during the hostilities. When it turned to the SP for aid in the face of increasing costs due to damages as well as shipping inefficiencies caused by the struggle, the North American giant rebuffed its subsidiary. "Your call for additional capital something of a thunderbolt," wired SP President William Sproule to Titcomb on September 17, 1926. "Our people not disposed to make any new committments [sic] at present."[30]

The Mexican government provided little help either, as it refused to compensate the SP de Mex for damages suffered during the conflict. The three-year state of siege seriously impacted Mexican finances, with expenses related to the conflict absorbing a staggering 45 percent of the national budget.[31] What little help the government and railroad provided each other was reciprocal. This mutual assistance came in the form of on-the-line protection from the troops riding the trains. In turn, the railroad moved them efficiently and rapidly to trouble spots. Twice-weekly passenger traffic was established as of the first week of April, 1929, and the entire month of April proved relatively calm.

The physical geography of the region played a central role in the ultimate defeat of the Cristeros. The plateaus of Jalisco, Michoacán, and surrounding areas, where the heaviest fighting took place, were rolling and gentle, broken only by low hills. Troops brought in by rail could thus easily reach the Cristeros, via the SP de Mex as well as on three other Mexican lines crossing through the area.[32]

In light of these events it is remarkable that the line turned the greatest profits of its history in 1928 and 1929. The company realized annual net profits of $377,000 and $451,000 U.S.—its first in many years. Although they had seen a positive return on their investment for the first time in many years, the conflict left railroad officials deeply frustrated and dispirited by the difficulties of operating during the struggle. As one observer of foreign capital in Latin America has noted, "Totals of investments have a certain bloodless quality about them that mocks the life they conceal."[33] The three-year period from 1926 to 1929 included the confluence of the Cristero Rebellion, sporadic Yaqui agitation, and Mexican resentment over the 1927 threat of U.S. intervention in Nicaragua.

The railroad was becoming, as one author remarked, "a thorn in the soft side of the Southern Pacific."[34] Noted SP executive Paul Shoup to Titcomb on July 31, 1929: "Of course we do not wish to build or buy any more lines in Mexico." Yet the company continued doggedly on.

The Company Town of Empalme

The SP de Mex did not aggravate these group-related conflicts as much as it was caught up in them as a participant. However, the company did exacerbate its own differences from Mexican workers and culture during the 1923–1929 period. The organization of the town of Empalme, several kilometers north of Guaymas, provides an illustration of how the railroad separated itself from Mexican ways.

The SP had first established Empalme in 1908 as a settlement for workers on the then–Sonora Railway, and the town grew steadily in the following years. The company eventually built general shops, a roundhouse, and a train yard. It greatly expanded the facilities in 1909–1910, and then again in 1924–1925. By the mid-1920s, the SP de Mex shops at Empalme were the most complete and best equipped in northwestern Mexico, and crews there could rebuild an entire locomotive from the ground up, if necessary (fig. 5.1).[35]

Empalme provided many amenities not commonly available to the working class in northwestern Mexico, and by 1924 more than five hundred SP de Mex employees lived in the town. There were 312 tenant houses with electricity and running water, general shops, a railway club, a hotel, a commissary store and warehouse, a hospital, schools, a police station, a jail, and a park. There was a roundhouse, a yard, and a foundry; the SP de Mex company shop's powerhouse provided electrical power. The local Pacific Fruit Express operations

5.1 SP Car 3423 in the shop for maintenance. (Courtesy of Donald Duke, Golden West Books, San Marino, California)

included a refrigeration facility that provided ice for shipment of perishable goods headed northwards along the line by refrigerator cars (fig. 5.2). A newsletter, *El Matamosca*, was published locally.[36]

However, after 1920 the company split the community into firmly defined Mexican and American zones, with striking disparities between the residences and the lives of the Mexican workers and their North American counterparts. The description by one historian of Empalme shows how sharp a division existed between the company and its Mexican workers: "As 1920 approached the American colony was formed, and was for those privileged few. It was separated from the rest of the population by numerous spikes that blocked Mexican vehicles from passing into the [U.S.] zone; chains marked the stopping point for pedestrians. One day governor Plutarcho Elías Calles was visiting Empalme, and ordered the spikes and chains to be removed, although they slowly reappeared."[37]

Empalme is also described in this account as a superficially genteel

5.2 Pacific Fruit Express facility and SP de Mex company shops in Empalme, on Guaymas Bay in the state of Sonora, ca. 1925. The ice plant, the foundry, and the powerhouse are visible from left to right. (From the Houston Family Pictures collection; courtesy of William Kalt, Tucson, Arizona)

and civilized place, with Americans playing tennis (courts were for their exclusive use), and only English spoken. Tranquility appeared to be of paramount concern. In order to preserve the peace of the colony, Mexican owners of carts with wooden wheels were even required to soak the wheels in water at regular intervals so they would swell and thus muffle the noise from the metal spokes.

Other descriptions of Empalme note that the gringo employees had substantial homes, but that most Mexican workers lived in considerably smaller residences. Many resided in barracks that lacked even basic necessities. Company police maintained strict control over the *norteamericano* section.[38]

However, Mexican laborers working at Empalme occasionally agitated against the SP de Mex, as they did in 1927 in a strike protesting the firing of a fellow worker. The Mexican workers in the little community held their ground against the company. After several weeks, President Calles was called in to mediate, and the worker was reinstated. Shortly after the dispute was resolved, the company offered to give 50 percent pay for the time lost by workers, but the men insisted on "100 percent or nothing." They received nothing.[39]

Other images of romance and charm occasionally reinforced the mirage of tranquility and peace in the company town and obscured the disparities between Mexican and U.S. workers. Charlie Chaplin and his wife, Lillita McMurray, were married in Empalme in November 1924, at the height of Chaplin's career, briefly giving the tiny spot worldwide prominence. Ironically, the previous year Chaplin had finished a movie about escaping to Mexico. In one scene of that film—*The Pilgrim*—he runs down to the boundary between the countries and, seeing a gang of outlaws on the Mexican side and a lawman on the U.S. side, races along the border "with one foot in Mexico and the other in the United States"—an apt description of the SP de Mex itself, as well as of the company's general perceptions of business in Mexico and the United States respectively: justice and order versus injustice and disorder.[40] In any event, the marriage made worldwide headlines. "The town was not a paradise. But it looked like one," wryly remarked a Mexican observer.[41]

As a result of these clashes and interactions, the SP de Mex's own otherness and isolation grew more apparent. The distance of the railroad from Mexico City, particularly in the Sonora region where Empalme lay and where many of the struggles with regional groups took place, served to emphasize the railroad's—and the region's—differences from the rest of Mexico rather than their similarities. Mexican attitudes about the otherness of the Sonora region itself, stretching back to the colonial era, helped to reinforce government perceptions of the railroad as a foreign object by virtue of its residence on the Mexican frontier.

Isolation and distance had concrete effects on the line's Sonora operations. As a railroad outside the structure of the NRM, the SP de Mex received less support from, and had fewer obligations to, the government than did NRM lines. The company did not have to provide free mail service, pay certain tariffs, withhold income tax on salaries, or purchase materials from Mexican companies—all of which the government required of NRM lines.[42] Because of its unique status outside of the NRM and the lack of legislation before 1930 to tightly regulate labor, Calles's administration could not readily replace workers or administrators during the work stoppages stemming from Yaqui and Cristero depredations as well as from the conflict in Nicaragua.

Had lines under the NRM umbrella tried to stop work for up to six weeks at a stretch, as did the SP de Mex during its various conflicts with Yaquis and Cristeros, the government could have legally coopted the lines and staffed them with Mexican laborers and administrators. But because of the SP de Mex's place outside the NRM organization, the government did not take over operations when various factions disrupted the railroad. On the other hand, the company did not receive substantial assistance from the government, and the railroad suffered the consequences of lost revenue because of these stoppages.

In fact, the farther north that conflicts occurred involving the SP de Mex, the more the government simply left the railroad to fend for itself. The government never intervened in the Anti-Chino League's campaign against the railroad on the border, nor did it act to aid the railroad against the Yaquis—other than fighting the Yaquis to protect the country's president, who happened to be on the train, and by providing troops on the line as an act of self-interest. As in Brazil, the region far distant from the country's population center was more difficult to manage and so far removed from the capital as to seem like another world. But Mexico also differed from the Brazilian case—it bordered on a large and powerful nation that wielded its own set of influences on the Sonoran region.

The Empalme colony also specifically brought the railroad's con-questing attitudes towards Mexico into sharp relief, and laborers coming from the United States reinforced the company's attitudes. Noted one writer about U.S. workers seeking employment on the SP de Mex: "A Colt .45, an iron constitution, and a Spanish-English dictionary were frequently the only requirements for the job."[43]

The SP de Mex's desire to build a railroad empire seemed more and more blustering as the years advanced, as well as increasingly ineffective. It did not have the backing of its own government or even the support of the parent company. And in the coming decade, Mexican labor gains would further erode the SP de Mex's ability to regulate its workforce or its operations generally.

CHAPTER 6

An Island upon the Land

Labor Law, Tariffs, and the Isolation of the Southern Pacific of Mexico (1930–1939)

By 1930, Mexican railroads totaled 12,500 kilometers—the fourth-longest network in the hemisphere, behind the United States, Canada, and Argentina. However, the lines constituted the most evenly distributed rail system in the hemisphere, crisscrossing the country from the Isthmus of Tehuantepec to the U.S. border, and from Veracruz and Tampico to the west coast. As contributors to the successes of the Mexican Revolution, as factors in the country's economic and political gains, and as carriers of more than a billion passengers and eight million tons of goods per year, Mexico's railroads represented the country's triumphs as well as its struggles.

As the 1920s had progressed, labor played a larger and larger role in the country's increasing successes at regulating foreign railroads. Industrial workers saw their contributions as beneficial to the nation as a whole. And while attitudes of government leaders and the press about the value of foreign investment and presence had changed considerably between 1900 and 1930, the views of workers about the presence of non-Mexican companies had remained relatively stable. Comments about Porfirian labor attitudes towards the railroad still applied in 1930: "In the rhetoric and the actions of the industrial worker . . . in his bitter denunciation of the foreign influence in his land, the Mexican worker was expressing his consciousness of being Mexican. For whatever the reason, he saw his own fate bound up with the larger fate of the nation."[1]

What was the general makeup of railroad labor on the Southern Pacific of Mexico (SP de Mex; Ferrocarril Sud-Pacífico de México)

6.1 Engineer inspecting locomotive wheels, ca. 1950. (Courtesy of Donald Duke, Golden West Books, San Marino, California)

line? The company used two distinct types, as did railroads in the National Railways of Mexico's (NRM; Ferrocarriles Nacionales de México) system. The first consisted of employees or subcontractors' employees working to construct (or reconstruct, as was so often the case with the SP de Mex's efforts) the actual railroad trackage and structures, including the laying of ties and rails as well as dynamiting and digging to create tunnels, laying foundations for bridges, and constructing ancillary buildings. The second type included the labor used to run and maintain the trains themselves and consisted of not only engineers, firemen, and conductors, but also a wide range of other classes of labor, including welders, tin workers, mechanics of various grades, electricians, carpenters, station employees, and other support personnel. Many of these men worked on the engines and cars in the well-equipped machine shops at Empalme and Guadalajara, while others worked strictly along the line, helping maintain the trains during their daily runs (fig. 6.1). Still other workers labored as ticket clerks and at various white-collar positions in the passenger stations dotting the line.

After the company completed construction of the line in 1927, it employed about four hundred men and women. This labor force, comprised of workers of both U.S. and Mexican nationality, soon found itself in the midst of a maelstrom of controversy. After 1930, Mexican law increasingly improved Mexican workers' rights and working conditions. At the same time, it lessened the rights of foreign workers in the country. SP de Mex officials strongly opposed these labor law changes, feeling that the effects would cause unreasonable financial hardship for the company. The largely judicial nature of the conflict meant that the SP de Mex's labor struggles were not primarily fought in pitched battles with angry workers. Rather, the fights took place in an oddly genteel but sometimes-heated series of conferences, legal encounters, telegrams, and late-night meetings.

Just as Mexico was starting to institutionalize the revolution through formation of the National Revolutionary Party (PNR; Partido Nacional Revolucionario) and the Institutional Revolutionary Party (PRI; Partido Revolucionario Institucional), the country was also beginning to institutionalize aspects of its interactions with U.S. investment after 1929. The Federal Labor Law of 1931, unveiled dramatically by the government via a banner headline in *Excélsior*, provided a powerful mechanism for control over foreign corporations, because it dictated how employers must treat their workers. The law had as its primary purpose the clarification of Article 123 of the 1917 Mexican Constitution: "making [Article 123] simple and certain in its application," as one newspaper article noted.[2] The new law, and its announcement, had a strong and stark impact on the SP de Mex.

The Federal Labor Law of 1931

Aarón Sáenz, secretary of industry, commerce, and labor, and one of the primary drafters of the legislation, addressed the sixth annual session of the Seminar on Mexico on the national value of the new labor law. Speaking on July 10, 1931, he began by discussing the not-yet-fully-realized Article 123: "Our Federal Constitution approved in the year 1917, in Article 123, establishes, as a basic principle, the right of workers

... to organize syndicates in defense of their legitimate interests. . . . It is worth noticing that Mexico was the first to consider the question of labor of such importance that it was made a matter of special and minute attention in the political Constitution of the country."[3]

Not only was a Mexican government leader attempting to build on the Constitution that Mexicans identified as the very heart of Mexico, but he was appealing to notions of patriotism by implying that Mexico had won some kind of race by being the first to give labor such prominence. In his lengthy speech, Sáenz (who had business ties to President Plutarco Elías Calles, the two men having established a construction firm together) also pointed to other ways in which Mexico was unique and why a new Mexican law (rather than adoption of some foreign version of labor law) was thus justified: "Considering these circumstances, the collective contract which in Mexico, due to the peculiarities of our industrial life, has acquired special characteristics somewhat different from those inherent in other countries, is minutely outlined in the proposed labor law."[4]

SP de Mex administrators were noticeably shaken by Sáenz' speech, which detailed extraordinary rights for workers, such as 75 percent pay when sick and three years' salary if permanently disabled. They referred to the speech frequently in their interoffice correspondence in the days following the speech.[5] To their dismay, railroad executives had no connections to, or sway over, the government-appointed committee drafting the new legislation. Even before the speech, they had obtained information about the provisions of the law and expressed their concern. "The situation looks rather discouraging," noted SP de Mex President Harvey B. Titcomb to Paul Shoup in mid-1931 at the end of a lengthy letter discussing the most radical features of the proposed law.[6] Shoup declared to Southern Pacific Company (SP) Chairman Hale Holden five weeks later that the proposed labor law was "as objectionable as anything ever proposed."[7]

The law was enacted on August 28, 1931, after passing rapidly through several committees for review and revision. Titcomb calculated the law's projected fiscal impact on the company. Article 111, for instance, stated that housing must be furnished for all employees, except in cities where the company employed less than one hundred men; Titcomb estimated a cost of 160,000 pesos annually. Other articles in the law called for an increase in the minimum wage, much higher payments for injured workers, and other cost-generating elements that the president calculated would total 1,167,000 pesos.[8]

Titcomb also expressed little trust in the Mexican government's management of the law. The final element on the president's tally sheet of expected expenses was 25,000 pesos for "Penalties." He remarked caustically that "the army of inspectors necessary to inspect; and enforce the provisions of this Labor Law will make a fertile field for the assessing of penalties on the slightest provocation, try as the company may to live within every rule and article of the Labor Law, and this alone will probably run into the annual amount of 25,000 [pesos]."[9]

Gone was the friendly aura of 1927 that had briefly followed the line's completion. In reality, the railroad faced conditions far less costly or difficult than those of 1923–1929. But the law made explicit what before had only been implicit: that the government had a virtually ironclad ability to control aspects of the SP de Mex's operations. The SP de Mex found the sensation highly uncomfortable. In a country where U.S. railroad officials could not buy politicians or manipulate other businesses, they were left to fend for themselves.

The SP de Mex held a certain work ethic that included the idea of not giving up easily, that hard work and business aptitude served as the most vital tools for corporate success. Officials continued to look on the bright side of a struggling business enterprise they might sensibly have abandoned twenty years earlier. Noted Shoup at the bottom of a brief note to Holden about Titcomb's estimates: "So many of these laws in Mexico are more honored in the breach than the observance, that, I do not feel the picture will necessarily be as black as is painted."[10] Holden agreed. "From the excessive length and complexity of these enactments it is of course impossible here to obtain any intelligent understanding of the effect upon our situation in Mexico, but we have a lively interest in knowing what changes, if any, are involved and what new conditions we will have to confront."[11] Often reactive to, and clueless about, the workings of Mexican law, the railroad continued down its rocky path.

The NRM had also suffered its own setbacks in the late 1920s and early 1930s. In March 1931, several months before passage of the law, the NRM reduced its numbers considerably—between twelve thousand and fifteen thousand employees, by one estimate. But the government gained the cooperation of the powerful unions by providing discharged NRM employees with free land in the state of Guerrero.[12] Such actions helped to deflect criticism against the government by the workers, paved the way for passage of the law in the face of layoffs, and illustrated the government's desires and success in appeasing Mexican labor.

Once Mexican leaders had instituted the new law, they continued to elevate Mexican objectives over foreign ones. Earl B. Sloan, chief engineer of the SP de Mex, wrote to Sáenz to complain about certain elements of the law. Sáenz had his chief clerk, Enrique Ortiz, pen the response:

> The subject matter of the Labor Law, due to the nature thereof, is a matter of public order and, possibly of national order, consequently, its precepts are of strict and immediate application . . . public and national interests have priority over private interests. . . . The ideas which the Government of the Nation maintains on the subject [are that] efforts are directed towards improving the situation of their own citizens, before that of foreigners.[13]

Mexican government officials were now expressing an explicit set of priorities. Railroad law acted as a powerful arbiter of Mexican life, labor constituted a vital element to the country, and foreign railroad interests took a distinct back seat to the interests of the nation. The days of Porfirian-driven U.S. railroad dominance had passed, as had the passive government attitudes towards the SP de Mex during the revolution and the subsequent railroad diplomacy the government practiced towards the company in the 1920s. These varying and often-clouded attitudes about how to treat the railroad had been decisively replaced with unambivalent expressions of Mexican sovereignty.

The most explicitly nationalist aspect of the new law, and the one that caused the most conflict between the government and the railroad, was Article 175. This stipulated that all workers in certain railroad categories be Mexican, if Mexican workers were available for the positions, "except in positions of direction." The railroad was forced to immediately get rid of fifty-seven American employees, some of whom had served with the line since it was the Sonora Railway. Emotions ran high. Struggling to obey the terms of the law, the railroad protested stiffly to the government and requested a clearer definition of "positions of direction."

Employees who had lost their jobs wrote impassioned letters to company officials, urging them to find positions on SP lines in the United States. Several sued the railroad. Some workers suggested removing Mexican employees from SP lines in retaliation. "There are, we believe, many positions on the Southern Pacific System which are at present filled by Mexican citizens and without mailice [sic] we suggest that it would be entirely equitable to permit us to displace such Mexicans in accordance with our ability to handle the work," wrote one group of workers.[14]

The company did find some workarounds to elements of the labor law by simply calling what appeared to be one thing, something else. For instance, the new law specified that doctors working in hospitals had to be Mexican. Noted Titcomb: "[This] makes necessary that any doctor performing hospital work be Mexican, therefore, title of Chief Surgeon Harris has been changed to Manager of Hospitals."[15]

But as important as the railroad law was to Mexican labor's future —it would prove to be the bedrock foundation for all future Mexican labor law up to the present day—the law was not the only element contributing to the railroad's increasing difficulties in the 1930s. Ironically, the other critical factor contributing to the company's decline had its origins in the United States rather than in Mexico—the Smoot-Hawley Tariff Act of June 1930. A device aimed at furthering economic nationalism in the United States, it caused a cascade of events leading to a bitter strike that culminated in the forced resignation of the president of the SP de Mex, Harvey B. Titcomb.

The SP de Mex Strike of 1932

The Great Depression hit the United States late in 1929 following the stock market crash. By early 1930, once the scope of the crisis had become apparent, President Herbert Hoover urged tariff reform and supported passage of the Smoot-Hawley Tariff Act, introduced by Sen. Reed Smoot of Utah and Sen. Willis C. Hawley of Oregon. Hoover signed the act into law on June 17, 1930. But other factors besides the Great Depression also contributed to passage of the act. For example, designed to help alleviate the poor economic conditions U.S. farmers had experienced throughout much of the 1920s, the law specifically taxed agricultural products entering the United States.

Unfortunately for the SP de Mex, the U.S. government considered the railroad legally to be a foreign corporation, even though a powerful North American company owned the line. The railroad carried large quantities of agricultural produce and goods north into the United States, and the tariff was designed to stop just this kind of flow. It was a protectionist tariff on goods, not on corporations, and the incidental nature of the SP de Mex's ties to its parent company in the United States provided no help at all. The law immediately raised import duties on vegetables a whopping 600 percent and had a dramatic impact on the SP de Mex. Shipments dropped from a peak of 8,394 carloads in 1929–1930 down to a low of 1,282 carloads by 1933–1934.[16] While the loss of this valuable produce traffic was offset somewhat by increased interchange business with the NRM through Guadalajara, the shipping situation looked particularly bleak.

Vegetables exported to the United States and Canada made up a large percentage of the railroad's business. Because they were picked and shipped almost exclusively during the first four months of the year, the company's profitability would typically soar for those four months, then drop into the red for the next eight months. For instance, in 1930, the railroad showed a gross profit at year's end of only 82,855 pesos, despite having earned 1,074,766 pesos by the end of May. Thus, the railroad's profitability (or its ability to remain solvent most years) depended very much on a successful four-month shipping season of winter and spring vegetables. And by the end of 1931, when the company realized total income of only 437,442 pesos throughout the year, due primarily to the effects of the Smoot-Hawley Tariff Act, it decided to take drastic measures. Salaries, as the company's largest expense, were the first items to be scrutinized and then cut.

To help the company's balance sheet and keep the firm viable, SP de Mex officers voluntarily accepted a salary cut of 10 percent, effective on January 1, 1932. On June 1, these salaries, which had for years been paid in U.S. dollars, were converted into Mexican currency at the rate of 2.65 pesos per dollar. Because the actual exchange rate of pesos to dollars at the time was about 3.65 pesos per dollar, the scale of salaries paid to SP de Mex officials was considerably lower than that paid to NRM officials and resulted in a total savings to the company of closer to 30 percent.

The Federal Labor Law of 1931 combined with the Smoot-Hawley Tariff Act to contribute to the railroad's financial woes, and the salary cost-cutting measures proved insufficient. During 1932 the company closed its offices at Mazatlán and Empalme, closed both of its branch lines, and consolidated the Sonora and Sinaloa divisions, permanently laying off many more U.S. employees.[17] At the same time, the company asked the remainder of its laborers—primarily workers of Mexican nationality—to voluntarily accept a wage cut of 10 percent and stated its intention of petitioning the Federal Board of Conciliation and Arbitration to make the reduction legal in the eyes of Mexican law. As feared, the employees struck, because to accept the SP de Mex's cut would mean relinquishing the higher pay scales of the powerful railroad unions.

The strike began on June 27, 1932. Government officials locked the safes and offices at the company's Guadalajara headquarters, and "the employees generally acted as though it were a fiesta occasion."[18] The U.S. consulate in Mazatlán, five hundred kilometers upline from Guadalajara, noted that "the strikers were wild with joy; they rang the church bells, and celebrated in a manner customary for this class of people, in the belief that they had won the strike."[19] And so they had, at least for the moment.

But the strike caused hardships along the line. A number of the small towns along the railroad depended on the line for the daily supply of some basic foodstuffs as well as water, and the dangers of their being without food and water grew steadily during the month-long strike (fig. 6.2). It was the first time that the entire line had been shut down for such a long period. Many in government and inside the SP believed resolution would be swift, as it sometimes was in Mexican

6.2 Car stopped at Esqueda, spring 1958. The railroad's presence spurred small businesses along the line, primarily in the form of food vendors. The water and fuel used by the railroad were owned by the SP de Mex. (Courtesy of Donald Duke, Golden West Books, San Marino, California)

railroad strikes, but the days turned into weeks without settlement. Calles was out of the country for most of the strike (he was with his wife, who was in the United States receiving medical attention), and although Ortiz Rubio (1930–1932) was president, it was felt that Calles's return was necessary to hasten the strike's end.

But Calles's presence back in Mexico City in mid-July and his subsequent efforts to mediate the strike did not persuade labor leaders to end the dispute. President Rubio decided to take unilateral action. He announced that, while the strike was legal, the public's rights demanded that service be resumed. Rubio immediately ordered trains to run, "without injury" to the rights of the strikers, and, if necessary, for the government itself to completely take over the railroad to ensure its continued operation. When the labor junta announced that it would be at least two weeks before the most vital issues of the strike could be settled amongst its leaders, the government took over the line on July 23. The new law made it now possible to do what it could not during previous disruptions such as the work stoppages due to the Nicaragua crisis, the Yaqui depredations, and the Cristero Rebellion: coopt the line and temporarily nationalize it.

SP de Mex railroad officials showed no consternation about the government takeover, but rather expressed relief. Company leaders provided the government with full information about line operations and did not push the government to set a date for return of line operations to corporate hands. The incident provided a kind of dry run for full Mexican control of the country's railroads by offering a test-case example for the government, which would not begin any large-scale takeovers of foreign properties until 1938 under President Lazaro Cárdenas (1934–1940). Railroad operations ran smoothly under the government while the ongoing labor dispute was arbitrated. The government had successfully shifted the locus of control of the railroad to itself, with the tacit approval of the SP de Mex.

Both sides hammered out their demands and placed them before an arbitration committee jointly chosen by the railroad and the government. Along with a variety of peripheral issues, four items were on the table, two for each side. Mexican labor demanded that, first, Titcomb be removed from office and, second, that the company pay for wages lost by workers during the month-long strike. For its part, the company requested the right to reduce wages and salaries by 10 percent, as it had originally desired and, second, the right to dismiss 183 Mexican employees in the Maintenance of Way department whose services were no longer needed.

Under the direction of Primo Villa Michel, the new secretary of industry, commerce, and labor who succeeded Sáenz in 1932, the commission studied both sides' requests and, on December 3, rendered a decision. The SP de Mex was absolved from paying wages lost during the strike and was also authorized to use foreigners in supervisory positions—both secondary requests made by the railroad in the arbitrations. However, arbiters denied the company's two most important claims—the right to dismiss the 183 unnecessary employees and to reduce wages—because "it is felt that these demands are not necessary for the life and maintenance of their business," as the *Excélsior* noted.[20]

Titcomb, the sacrificial lamb who spoke so little Spanish that he needed an interpreter whenever meeting with Mexican officials even after living in Mexico for five years, fell by the wayside as labor demands for his resignation were met. Article 33 of the Mexican Constitution noted that "undesirables" could be expelled from the country, and Mexico used this legal mechanism to justify removing Titcomb in order to meet the demands of Mexican labor.

The reasons for Mexican labor's dislike of Titcomb remain unclear. Labor leaders may have felt him to be a major obstacle to reaching resolution with the railroad over the strike; he may also have struck a personally discordant note. Titcomb received anonymous threats to dynamite his private car and, at age 61, quietly acquiesced to Mexican demands after losing the arbitration, left the company, and retired.[21] He was immediately replaced by Walter Douglas, who had served for many years as an official of the SP. The federal government, which had no desire to assume the financial burden of running the line, ran the trains only until September 23, returning control to the SP de Mex at that point.

The Federal Labor Law of 1931 and the Smoot-Hawley Tariff Act had taken their toll on the railroad. Still, the line's administrators gamely pushed ahead. The Mexican government had gained distinct regulatory and judicial control over the railroad. But these legal mechanisms were not the only ways in which the government, as well as the workers on the line, maintained and demonstrated Mexican sovereignty. Other forms of control also appeared.

Forms of Mexican Resistance to SP de Mex Desires

Mexico used two particularly effective forms of resistance to counteract the wishes of SP de Mex officials regarding labor. First, government leaders appeased railroad executives by making unkept promises and vague assurances about future events in which the railroad had a stake. Second, laborers themselves resisted foreign corporate pressures by expressing their own cultural and social norms.

Calles in particular had no problems in keeping SP de Mex officials at bay over issues of labor, placating them with generalizations and platitudes. Meeting with Calles in July 1933, SP de Mex President Douglas noted that "the General's attitude in connection with all our matters is one of deep sympathy and cooperation and he assures me that he is determined . . . to assist in every way possible to make the enterprise a financial success." Douglas found the promises and the atmosphere heady: "This trip has had the . . . advantage for me of bringing me into close personal contact with the man who will probably be the next president. We have practically been together every day for nearly two weeks, and I have, therefore, had an excellent opportunity of knowing him . . ."[22]

But the taciturn Calles provided virtually nothing in the way of quantifiable assistance to the railroad in the next several years. Termed "the president of the workers," Calles had no desire to antagonize the well-organized and rapidly growing organized labor sector that had supported him in his earlier term.[23] Finally reduced to meeting with Calles's private secretary, a woman named Cholita (described by one historian as "an efficient and mysterious girl who was utterly devoted to him"[24]), SP official Holden reported:

On Saturday night I took supper with Cholita, private secretary to General Calles, at her house, and I had a long talk with her with reference to our controversies before the Board of Conciliation and Arbitration, whose decisions, as I told her, were being largely dictated by Lic. Portes Gil. . . . She said the only solution was to have someone represent the company who had more political influence than the Syndicato (Union); that obviously there was no question of the attitude of the Government or of General Calles towards the company, but that it would be impossible to have our friends continually bothered with our matters in detail which, while they meant a good deal to us, were of no great importance to the government. . . . I am due for an appointment with the General myself, but will not bother him in his present ill condition . . .[25]

Cholita's suggestion was laughable because of its inherent impossibility: no one inside or outside SP de Mex ranks could have had more political influence on Gil or Calles than the intensely nationalistic unions, whether the largest of the unions, the Confederación de Trabajadores de México (CTM), the newly formed but powerful Sindicato de Trabajadores Ferrocarriles de la República Mexicana (STFRM), the Confederación Regional Obrera Mexicana (CROM), or the Confederación General de Trabajadores (CGT). All of these groups had substantial influence with the government because of their increasing political strength on the eve of Cárdenas's election. While the letter illustrates the government's willingness to let railroad officials into its intimate circle and to express sympathy and support, it also shows how members of this circle gently pushed the SP away and how hopefully—perhaps wishfully—the SP swallowed the sweetened medicine of rejection. For Mexico, defense of Mexican sovereignty could take a number of successful forms—in this case, through kind words and delaying tactics.

The second form of resistance was offered by laborers themselves. After construction had been completed in 1927, most of the foreign workers imported from Utah and elsewhere left the project, their contract work finished. The railroad felt that it could attract a nearly unlimited supply of laborers in the form of poorly paid campesinos from the ranchos and haciendas on the lands through which the line would run. However, in practice, the company had difficulty maintaining a sufficient supply of workers.

Because the railroad's wages far exceeded what workers could otherwise make through local employment, many of the company's laborers would put in only three or four days of work and then stop for protracted periods of time.[26] This on-again, off-again mode wreaked havoc with the railroad's carefully orchestrated payroll and, during construction, made it difficult to accurately estimate when certain sections of track would be completed. But as Jonathan C. Brown has pointed out, "The Mexican's time-honored ethos consisted of entering and leaving the workplace of his own free will—not the employer's."[27] For Mexican laborers on the SP de Mex, this ability to control their environment reduced the effectiveness of the railroad in transporting goods and passengers because the line's administrators could not consistently dictate or control the workers' schedules.

SP de Mex management harped perpetually about the quality of Mexican workers. For instance, a 1938 letter from Douglas to A. D. McDonald, Chairman of the executive committee of the SP, noted that "the condition in the General Office is so bad that clerks consistently absent themselves from their duties for the greater part of the day and do their work after six o'clock so as to be paid double salary for overtime."[28] But as Brown has noted, skilled workers in Mexico combated the pressures on their lifestyle and culture: "They did not so much resist the penetration of capital as agitate against changes that capitalism seemed to demand in their lives. Individual choice, leisure time, use of the employer's property, working-class cultural solidity: these were traditions the Mexicans considered worthy of preservation in the new industrial order."[29]

The structure and maturity of Mexican railroad labor after 1930 provided a rare opportunity for resistance against North American railroads by Mexican railroad workers and an accompanying expression of anti–U.S. solidarity. Mexican nationals working for the SP de Mex refused to act as the kind of employees desired by railroad administrators: servile, efficient, and dependent. Their reluctance to maintain the work ethic imposed by their foreign employers, and their strikes and union agitation, all provided active mechanisms through which to show this unwillingness.

Issues of Legal Treatment

Along with the SP de Mex's traumas with the Smoot-Hawley Tariff Act, the Federal Labor Law of 1931, and the 1932 strike and subsequent government takeover, it also had to contend with the law requiring a 10 percent tax on the company's gross revenue. That tax on the gross income of all railroads operating in Mexico had been first levied by the government via a 1923 executive order. Issued by President Alvaro Obregón just as the SP had begun construction work to close the line between Tepic and La Quemada, that order declared that all railroad companies, whether domestic or foreign, would pay a tax upon all income generated by passengers, freight, storage, and deliveries.[30]

The SP felt the tax was unfair for two reasons. First, its introduction had seemed arbitrary to officials, who saw no reason to turn over a tenth of the company's revenue to the government. Second, the Mexican government still owed the railroad payments in the form of bonds for depredations suffered in both the Mexican Revolution and the Cristero Rebellion. In the course of their interactions with the government over the issue of payment of the tax, railroad administrators demonstrated what seemed to be a poor grasp of the motivations and workings of Mexican law. The company continued to play a frustrated but passive role in the drama of the line's treatment by the Mexican government:

> We seem to be approaching a crisis of some character in these matters . . . I have no doubt our Mexican counsel are able and giving us good advice, but I do not know them and do not understand the atmosphere around Mexican court proceedings where the government is so directly interested as in these matters, and how sound legally our former arrangements through Ex-President Obregón . . . may be. We seem to have in effect certain laws and decrees to the contrary. Therefore it is somewhat puzzling to know how a Mexican court can be expect [sic] to uphold our position in the face of the attitude of the present administration in power.[31]

Alternately hopeful and frustrated with the Mexican government over the 10 percent tax, the railroad paid the assessment throughout the years as requested, although under protest. "The conflict continues," tersely noted one SP de Mex memo in 1932 discussing the legal necessity of steady payments. Part of the reason Mexico would not allow for more lenient or flexible terms of payment of the 10 percent tax, as it had done with American oil companies, was because Alberto J. Pani, former head of the National Constitutional Railroads (NCR; Ferrocarriles Constitucionalistas de México), was now serving as the Minister of Finance, and he adamantly opposed any financial conciliation with the company. The intensely nationalistic Pani was no more sympathetic to foreign railroads in 1932 than he had been in 1916.[32] U.S. oil companies warranted a more diplomatic response from Mexico because the government made far more money from Mexican oil than it did from the SP de Mex.

The railroad also received very little legal or political assistance from its own government after 1930. U.S. Ambassador J. Ruben Clarke, posted in Mexico City, noted to Secretary of State Henry L. Stimson that the railroad was on shaky ground in trying to extract money from the Mexican government: "We cannot (repeat not) properly make representation against . . . the new labor law or its application to American workmen. It is applicable to all railways not merely the Sud Pacífico. On abstract moral and equitable grounds we appear to have little basis for complaint in view of the eighty or ninety thousand Mexicans who have been thrown out of employment in the United States and who have been forced to return to Mexico."[33]

In the face of both corporate and U.S. governmental reluctance to push for the more lenient terms of tax payment that oil companies had received, Mexico continued to pursue the railroad over a variety of other tax and legal issues, large and small, throughout the 1930s. Sometimes Mexican attacks on the SP de Mex constituted pure harassment. For instance, between 1932 and 1941, the government assessed duties on SP de Mex trains entering the country with U.S. fuel oil. In doing so, the Mexican government attempted to fine the railroad for the relatively minuscule quantities of oil and fuel used to lubricate and run the locomotives, leading the railroad to calibrate all of their instruments on trains to accurately measure how much oil and fuel the locomotives had consumed each time they crossed into or out of Mexico.[34]

In looking about for reasons they had met with these forms of judicial and financial treatment in Mexico, the railroad also targeted its own legal department. "We lack competent and adequate legal advice, but I think our own organization in Titcomb, Sloan and Stark is quite effective, which relieves my mind of one doubt I had," remarked Douglas to Hugh Neill, secretary and vice president of the SP in January 1932. And again in May, Shoup noted that "there is something to be desired in connection with our legal representation."[35]

These frustrations with law, along with roadblocks in the form of politicians and unions, contributed to SP de Mex failures. In addition, interpersonal elements of doing business in Mexico contributed to the railroad's downfall. By mid-decade, still puzzled over their lack of success, administrators hired a consultant to provide a "big-picture" overview of why they had gone so wrong in Mexico.

The 1936 Consultant's Report to the Railroad

In 1936, an unidentified consultant sent a detailed proposal to Mr. S. K. Burke, assistant vice president of the SP.[36] The proposal identified specific elements in the SP de Mex's declining fortunes and suggested solutions to the Mexican subsidiary's steadily worsening situation. The report covered the years 1930 through 1935 and pointed out that once the line had been completed through to Guadalajara in 1927, freight traffic through Nogales and Naco declined sharply. The decline, noted the report, was not the result of any decreased business handled by the SP de Mex, but rather was due to loss of business to NRM lines going farther south into Mexico via Guadalajara and through various Pacific ports in Mexico such as Manzanillo.

In 1929, for instance, the SP de Mex interchanged 86.7 percent of its tonnage with the SP at the border, and 13.3 percent with the NRM at Guadalajara. But by 1935, the percentage of freight crossing the U.S. border to the SP had dropped to 26.8 percent, and the NRM connection to the SP de Mex at Guadalajara was receiving 73.2 percent of the line's freight business. Mexico was benefiting from the increased traffic, while the SP de Mex—and the SP—were suffering from the decrease.

Four reasons existed for this decline, noted the report. First, there was a "failure of trade"—a concept the report attempted to elaborate on by somewhat vaguely describing it as "a barrier of indifference" between the markets of the west coast of Mexico and the United States. Second, agents of European and Asian countries—specifically, Japan and Germany—were somehow disturbing traffic through various unspecified "endeavors." These foreign agents were "ready to conform to Mexican business methods," noted the report, implying that the SP de Mex was itself not ready or able to conform to those methods. Third, representatives of the NRM had successfully solicited Mexican business away from the SP de Mex. Fourth, and most tellingly, the company lacked knowledge about market conditions on the west coast of Mexico. It had a poor understanding of the natural resources of the region, as well as a general lack of comprehension of customs procedures, embargoes, and tariff matters.

The report placed the blame for the failure of trade between Mexico and the United States on the shoulders of the SP de Mex for its inability to understand Mexican businesses, shippers, and traders, an understanding that would have "enabled the traders of the United States and those of Mexico, unalike in temperament and accustomed to different methods and practices of business," to transact business under conditions satisfactory to both. "To the Mexican mind," the report continued, "the business methods of the United States are quite incomprehensible and constitute a rather elaborate code of incivility and rudeness. "On the other hand," the report noted, "the irresponsible natures and dilatory practices of the Mexicans are a source of extreme annoyance to the traders of the United States." Given these differing attitudes, observed the report, business efforts would inevitably be stymied. The report pointed to a "barrier of indifference" arising between the two countries' attitudes about trade, exacerbated by the diminishment of value of the SP de Mex to the parent company as a feeder property.

The report placed high value on interpersonal abilities, pointing to Japanese and German agents as "intelligent, considerate agents, whose business it is to encourage agriculture and manufacturing and the stimulation of trade, and who, above all else, in their dealings with the Mexicans are careful to avoid offense" and blamed the steadily mounting tonnage flowing south from Guadalajara instead of through the U.S. border on the efficacy of the methods employed by these agents. Surprisingly, the effects of the Great Depression on the United States and on Mexico were not given much credence. "With some inconsequent modification admittedly due to general world conditions and to internal conditions in Mexico," the report noted, "the factors enumerated above have been controlling in the sustained decline of freight traffic through Naco and Nogales."

The report suggested a fix for the woes of declining freight revenues. The most heavily stressed suggestion was to hire a special representative who would split time between the SP lines in the United States and the SP de Mex. This person's sole job would be to restore the former importance of the Mexican line. This agent, suggested the report, would serve as a sort of cheerleader for the company, lecturing on conditions of trade in the west coast of Mexico, on "the temperament of the people," and other elements of life and business in Mexico. In the process, he would "successfully sell the West Coast area to the traders of the United States." The report also urged that this representative be responsible for "the writing of articles on West Coast commodities for trade magazines" in the United States, as well as for issuing a monthly bulletin of trade, crop, and market conditions in Mexico, including commentaries on legislative matters touching upon SP interests on the west coast.

The final suggestion for the duties of this key liaison was "to carefully avoid anything that might be interpreted as an invitation to American capital to invest in Mexico." This oblique reference can be interpreted in several ways: first, that the SP did not want to invite business competition into Mexico; or second, and more likely, that the SP was reluctant to antagonize Mexican politicians and businessmen through a blatant push for more American involvement in Mexico, given the steadily growing anti–U.S. nationalist spirit evident under both Calles and Cárdenas.

The stereotypical tone of the report about the nature of Mexicans and "the Mexican mind" may have reinforced the railroad's own prejudices about Mexico. However, the basic suggestion of focusing on interpersonal elements and striving to understand Mexican culture was sound. Tellingly, the SP de Mex did nothing to implement the suggestions related to develop a better understanding of Mexico. Rather than looking inward to forces it could control somewhat— such as the enthusiasm and focus of its own administrators—it turned outward to largely unproven revenue sources such as tourism to try to keep the line viable.

Tourism and the SP de Mex

Although SP and SP de Mex officials had expressed nascent enthusiasm for the benefits that tourism could bring to the Mexican line as early as 1926, and the railroad published promotional materials in 1929, the company made no concerted effort to promote tourism until 1935. In that year, the company decided that building a tourist hotel along the coast, as well as more vigorously promoting tourist destinations along the line, might help greatly in the railroad's quest to generate profits.

In 1936, the railroad completed construction of the Hotel Playa de Cortés. The ambitious resort was located five kilometers north of Guaymas, along an isolated stretch of coastline. The line provided easy reach to this previously inaccessible stretch of beach for visitors, and the railroad promoted it heavily. The resort was at the tail end of what had historically been a very stable, reliable, and relatively undisturbed stretch of track.

The thirty-room hotel opened for business on March 5, 1936. It depended on fishing as its principal attraction, although visitors could also wander the grounds and gardens, swim in the hotel's saltwater pool, play golf and tennis, or hunt in the nearby hills. Near the hotel was Bacochibampo Bay, which provided excellent shallow-water fishing, while the hotel's own boats took visitors out for more extensive deep-water fishing as well. The warm waters of the Gulf of California produced large swordfish, sharks, rays, tuna, dolphin, albacore, and rock bass. The hotel apparently got off to a good start; new boats were purchased several times to meet the increasing tourist demand. Three boats initially made up the fleet, which eventually expanded to include fourteen craft.[37]

Travel to Playa de Cortés was not the only substantial tourist traffic the railroad handled. Mazatlán, Guadalajara, and Mexico City were also promoted as tourist destinations best reached via the SP de Mex. Tourism seemed as if it would finally provide some economic stability and success to the railroad. Even in late 1935, despite agitated strikes and other destructive railroad activities on the line and the presidential struggle for power between Calles and Cárdenas, Douglas noted to

Holden several months before the opening of the Hotel Playa de Cortés:

> I am glad to advise you that the effect of the burning of our bridges in Sonora and the general disturbed condition in Mexico does not seem to have discouraged the tourist traffic and, in fact, our passenger business is showing a gratifying increase. In the first week in December we handled by districts 3862 more commercial passengers than in the same period of 1934, and for the second week in December 2570 more.[38]

Numbers such as these were encouraging to upper management and helped to validate their decision to complete the hotel. The SP de Mex began actively promoting its line to tourists in 1936, targeting potential visitors to its hotel and other tourist destinations. They apparently made no effort to advertise to Mexican tourists, but rather put their promotional efforts into bringing U.S. tourists into the country. They thus deprived themselves of a golden opportunity to generate tourist revenue.

The company advertised until 1941, by which time the company had lost virtually all motivation to be in Mexico and its promotional efforts trickled to nothing. *Sunset Magazine* ran the largest number of the company's ads—approximately forty during the six-year period. The railroad also widely circulated promotional brochures. "You don't need to know Spanish," remarked one such flier written in the first person as an anecdotal account of travel on the line, which went through seven printings during the decade. "Naturally, I had some ideas about Mexico before I left. They were all wrong."

In some ways, these brochures and ads echoed the company's attitudes about, and experiences in, Mexico. "Go while the West Coast is still unspoiled," noted one 1933 advertisement, implying that affairs along the coast would change for the worse in some unspecified way. This was a far cry from an 1897 brochure published by the Sonora Railway to entice tourists. "Vamos á México," the Porfirian-era blurb noted after talking about Hernán Cortés' conquest of Mexico. "It is not probable that you may wear your welcome out." Perhaps unconsciously, but distinctly paralleling their increasing difficulties and pessimism about doing business along the west coast, the SP de Mex reflected changing attitudes about how welcome it felt in the country. "It's OK to visit, but do so now; we certainly don't plan on staying!" the company seemed to be saying after 1930. Still, the company also illustrated its attraction to the country in a small way in this 1933 brochure: "Mexico has a personality . . . so poignant . . . that it sinks deep, deep into your consciousness. You can never forget Mexico."[39]

In 1945, after the hotel had fallen onto hard times, it received a letter from Conrad N. Hilton, the president of the Hilton hotel chain, offering to lease the hotel from the railroad for ten years at 10,000 pesos per year and to make 150,000 pesos in improvements. With breathtaking disingenuousness, Hilton noted in his letter to SP President Armand T. Mercier that "we realize that taking over the Guaymas Hotel may be more romantic than practicable from a money making standpoint, but on the other hand, we would expect to get a lot of pleasure out of its operation . . ."[40] The hotel had received about 1,700 paying guests in May 1943 and fewer than 1,500 in May 1945—reasonable numbers for a tourist hotel of its size, but not sufficiently profitable for a company that was already trying to extricate itself from business operations in Mexico.

SP de Mex: U.S. or Mexican Corporation?

In addition to its own sporadic self-identification as Mexican, the company felt that economic and legal advantages would accrue from having Mexico's legal agreement that the railroad was Mexican. During the revolution, the company had proudly and clearly identified itself as a foreign company, with a U.S. ideology and U.S. workers. But the railroad held a new attitude in the 1930s.

The question of who considered the SP de Mex a Mexican corporation, and when, had a bearing on whether or not the company was responsible for paying various taxes to Mexico. The government and the railroad persistently clashed over the issue of taxes between 1924 and 1931, and the railroad litigated against the government, although it paid the taxes as requested. The most important issue at hand with regard to national corporate status of the SP de Mex was that of car rentals. The government tried to tax railroad cars that the SP de Mex regularly rented from the SP, contending that the cars were U.S. property and thus taxable as foreign-owned items. The SP de Mex, however, disagreed, saying that it was precisely because the cars were mobile that they were not subject to ordinary taxes levied on property; the cars fell, the SP de Mex argued, into some other category than the normal one used to define industrial "machines" performing services in Mexico.

The railroad knew from experience that taking the government to court offered poor hopes for success. Thus, it tried the different tack of trying to obtain legal status from the government as a Mexican corporation and fought more and more vigorously after 1930 for recognition as such. It seemed as if it should have been an easy task. After all, Secretary of Finance José Ives Limantour's 1899 Railroad Law had contained an intensely nationalistic element that stated that railroads as well as their employees were considered to be Mexican in the eyes of Mexican law. Hilario Medina, Mexico's undersecretary of state, had elaborated on the intent of the law in a 1919 memo to George T. Summerlin, U.S. chargé d'affaires in Mexico:

> According to Article 49 of the mentioned [1899] Railway Law, enterprises shall always be Mexican even though the companies have been organized in foreign lands or some of their members are foreigners; they shall be subject to the courts of the Republic and they, as well as the foreigners and their successors who take part in the business as stockholders, employees, or others whatever their character, shall be considered as Mexicans in everything referring to them; they may never assert . . . any right growing out of their being foreigners under any pretext whatsoever . . .[41]

During the late Porfiriato, the revolution, and the 1920s, the company had resisted the idea of being legally Mexican. It not only steadily identified itself as U.S., but had also been proudly identified as such by the North American press. In the media's eyes, progress and completion of the railroad could only be attributed to U.S. persistence, capitalism, and engineering know-how. But by 1930, its situation and attitudes had changed considerably, and the company attempted to obtain explicit legal status from the courts as a Mexican corporation. Mexico City now resisted granting the company this status. Although the SP de Mex had incorporated as a U.S. corporation in New Jersey in 1909, Titcomb felt that the company was somehow Mexican by dint of having its headquarters in Mexico:

> If it is insisted upon that the SP de Mex is a New Jersey corporation and, therefore, foreign, which appears to us incredible, and which our attorneys consider not legal, it may mean that the National Railways will be forced to withhold the payment of rental of equipment, perdiem [sic], etc., of 6 percent of the money that they would pay the SP de Mex, which of course will make a serious decrease in our revenues.[42]

The issue of the SP de Mex's legality as a Mexican corporation ultimately died a slow but inexorable death. As the courts debated the issue, tension in company circles remained high: not only might the railroad owe the government current and back taxes, but if the company was legally Mexican, then salaries paid to employees of the line were also taxable under Mexican law, adding to the individual burdens shouldered by employees, most of whom had moved to Guadalajara in 1927. However, as Guy V. Shoup—Paul Shoup's older brother—noted in late 1931, "The legal opinions aren't very clear on the subject, but I suppose they are as clear as the situation permits."

Mexico never granted status as a Mexican corporation to the SP de Mex. In early 1934, the courts did drop the related matter of taxes on car rentals. Apparently, internal disagreements between the general auditor and other tax attorneys in the government were substantial enough that the Mexican government could not reach consensus. All parties finally quietly let the matter lie by the spring of 1934.[43]

Meanwhile, as the SP de Mex tried to gain advantages by wearing whichever national hat seemed appropriate, Mexican politicians acted inconsistently over the years about just what they considered a Mexican corporation and what they did not—and communicated legal opinions to the railroad whenever the issue arose. "As was stated to you in Oficio No. 14113 of October 10 of last year," noted M. J. Sierra, head of the Secretariat of Foreign Relations, contradicting the 1899

Railroad Law, "Mexican companies are only those which have been constituted in conformity with the Mexican Law and have their domicile in National Territory." Sierra noted that Mexican law did allow foreign corporations—including the SP de Mex—to be considered Mexican, but that if the company wished to do so, it would have to renounce the diplomatic protection of its government and its employees would have to consider themselves Mexican citizens.[44]

Mexico's changing attitudes about the nationality of foreign companies reflect the shift in Mexican views about sovereignty and the integration of foreign corporations into Mexican life. In 1899, amidst the heavy U.S. corporate presence pouring into Mexico, the law stating that "all enterprises shall always be Mexican even though the companies have been organized in foreign lands" gave Mexico a means to at least claim control over foreign concerns and rationalize the variety of ways in which they treated those concerns. But, in the 1930s, legal decisions explicitly demonstrated Mexico's intentions regarding foreign capital. Foreign enterprises were just that—foreign, and not Mexican. This clear delineation, although a 180-degree change in attitude from Porfirian views of foreign companies, allowed government leaders to exercise self-determination and control by excluding foreign companies rather than including them.

Increasing Strains between the SP and the SP de Mex

The SP and the SP de Mex maintained good business relations through most of the thirty-three years during which they were separate yet related companies. However, the parent company became more and more reluctant to aid its Mexican subsidiary during the 1930s as the company continued to lose money. The SP was concerned only with the SP de Mex's profitability and, on that score, the Mexican line fell far short of corporate goals and wishes.

The SP tried hard to support its Mexican subsidiary between 1909 and 1930, pouring in many millions of dollars over the years to bolster the line and make it profitable. But the Federal Labor Law of 1931 and the government takeover of the line in 1932 were nearly the last straw for both the SP and the SP de Mex, and a series of other events throughout the 1930s only added to the SP de Mex's woes. By 1939, the "Esspey," as it was often termed by the U.S. press, had invested a total of $54,298,000 U.S. in the line.[45] The SP managed to recoup some of its losses by depreciating $22 million U.S. over the years, but that action only halved the SP de Mex's indebtedness to its parent company.

The Great Depression exacerbated the increasingly strained relations between the two entities, primarily because of its effect on the parent company. Flattened freight and passenger revenues in the United States meant less income and tighter margins, and the North American giant began to stumble in its own operations.[46] Beginning in mid-decade, the SP began trying to push the smaller SP de Mex out of the nest with some vigor, to either fly or crash to the ground. In 1935, the parent company placed financial relations with its Mexican line on a cash basis; that is, it required that all transactions, bills, and vouchers be paid in cash rather than by credit, and the SP de Mex had to "pay as it went." Still willing to try life as an independent operation in Mexico, the SP de Mex cooperated rather than declaring bankruptcy. In 1934 and then again in 1943, the SP de Mex acquired about a third of the 750,000 shares of its own stock—some of it purchased from the SP, but most of it simply given to the subsidiary from the parent company without any cash changing hands.

Nationalization of the NRM

The final event that affirmed Mexico's ability to control and regulate its own lines and provided a clear rejection of foreign ownership of railroads in the country came in June 1937. That month, the Sindicato de Trabajadores Ferrocarrileros (STF) took over ownership of the NRM. Mexican control over railroad administration in the country reached its highest point. The move had the full support of President Lázaro Cárdenas and, in reality, simply strengthened government control of the NRM lines rather than transferring them to an autonomous union. The government and the STF had close ties; the union was in fact a quasi-government organization, tightly linked to the Cárdenas government.[47] An article in the *Diario Oficial*, the official daily government organ, described the arrangement thusly: "While the Government, in Article 10 of the Law [creating the administration of the railway] maintains some supervision and control in important matters, the work of administration is practically in the hands of the workers who are to elect a Board of Administration of seven members."[48]

The move allowed the government to confiscate the foreign-owned bonds and preferred stocks of the various lines under the NRM. *El Universal* noted that the move "institutionalized the revolution" and provided Mexico with a form of autonomy and self determination.[49] Citizens and stockholders in the United States expressed their outrage. "Good American dollars have been innocently invested in the building of that railway [the NRM system and the U.S.–owned railroads under its umbrella], without which Mexico would still be an Indian desert," proclaimed one man writing to the U.S. State Department.[50]

But now, in sharp contrast to typical responses to Mexican appropriation of U.S. properties during the revolution, some U.S. citizens conspicuously avoided even the suggestion of armed force in Mexico, preferring a good tongue-lashing instead. "A little good blunt American speech will bring reason to them," urged the correspondent. "We cannot pussy-foot with confiscators, thieves and selfish one-track-minded communists. Such tactics preclude good-neighborliness. Will you not do something?" Not really, seemed to be the U.S. response, as the U.S. State Department and the War Department urged restraint. The U.S. government did protest, but not with any great enthusiasm, nor did it make rumblings of armed intervention, as it had often threatened during the revolution.

Nationalization had a direct impact on the SP de Mex. Within six months, the NRM had stopped paying the SP de Mex fees for freight transferred to Mexican lines. By March 1938, the debt owed by the coopted national lines to the SP de Mex had reached a million pesos.[51] SP de Mex debts mounted even more rapidly. By late April 1938, the company owed Standard Oil $175,000 U.S. Administrators paid local debts and expenditures but allowed its stock, shops, equipment, and rolling stock to slowly deteriorate.

The U.S. vice consul in Guaymas sharply criticized the SP de Mex for its problems. "It is very sad but absolutely true that the management of the railway is almost wholly responsible for the railway's plight," noted A. F. Yepis. "The railway's chief lack is precisely trained and efficient personnel. . . . It almost appears that the management is endeavoring by all possible means to hasten the downfall of the railway, and it also appears that this is bound to happen in the very near future."[52]

The railroad's annual losses between 1935 and 1940 averaged more than $663,000 U.S.[53] As early as June 1938, *La Gaceta* in Guaymas declared that the company was "bankrupt."[54] A detailed internal evaluation by the firm in 1939 did not hold much hope out to the company for possible increases in revenue, particularly given the nationalized status of other lines in the country. Acting in the spirit of the report, the SP's executive committee recommended at the end of 1939 that Douglas, president of the SP de Mex, immediately offer the properties of his company for sale to the Mexican government.

President Cárdenas, however, declined the offer. The NRM was engaged in its own financial struggles, and the government's financial status, exacerbated by the cost of supporting an overabundance of well-protected Mexican railroad workers, left it with little money for acquisition of the line.[55]

The Final Decade

A series of strikes, severe inflation after World War II, and the failure of the railroad to generate sufficient tourist revenue caused continued deterioration of the SP de Mex's operations. Rolling stock continued to wear out and was not replaced. Trackage needing repairs went untended for longer and longer periods. Air and auto travel had also changed the importance of the railroad to the country. The country's air force could rapidly reach all corners of the country, and passengers could now reach the west coast by a highway that roughly paralleled the railroad.

Finally, in 1950, the company opened negotiations with the Mexican government to purchase the line. After lengthy discussions, government leaders agreed to buy the railroad for $12,000,000 U.S.—$3 million in cash and the rest in 3.5 percent bonds. This sum equaled less than the scrap value of the rails alone. Mexico took control of the railroad on December 21, 1951. In addition to right-of-way, tracks, and structures, the deal included ninety-three locomotives, one thousand freight cars, and eighty-eight passenger cars (fig. 6.3). A lengthy and involved foreign incursion into Mexico had come to an end. The line's president, Bernard S. Sines (known as "El Oso Polar"—the polar bear—by Mexican railroaders because of his preference for his air-conditioned car, which he rarely left) stayed on as interim manager for fifteen months.[56]

In the next two years, the Mexican government received a total of $67 million U.S. to rehabilitate the line—ironically, virtually all of it via a series of loans from U.S.–based institutions such as the Bank of America and the U.S. Import-Export Bank, as well as from the International Bank for Reconstruction and Development. Renamed the Ferrocarril Pacífico, the line acquired several branch lines, modernized its right-of-way, and was rediscovered by tourists and passengers in the 1960s. By 1975 more than 1,176,000 people rode the line annually. The line was not absorbed quickly into the NRM; instead, the government continued to run it for a number of years as a separate corporate entity. Finally, in 1987, the NRM absorbed the Ferrocarril Pacífico, bringing it under full government control at last.

The government's successes in using law effectively as a controlling mechanism stemmed not only from the comprehensiveness and solid implementation of regulations, but also from SP de Mex officials' inability to clearly understand the exigencies and subtleties of the workings of aspects of Mexico's legal system. Like the Mitre Law in Argentina in 1907, the Federal Labor Law of 1931 gave the government an efficient and effective means of regulating labor—the lifeblood of all railroads operating in Mexico. In the 1930s, Mexico improved its ability to arbitrate the country's economic and labor future, and the railroad suffered a corresponding loss in its capacity to aggressively pursue its own interests. Three players—the Mexican government, the U.S. government, and the SP de Mex itself—contributed to this decisive swinging of the nationbuilding versus foreign penetration equation in favor of Mexico.

The Mexican government played the largest role. The Federal Labor Law of 1931 strengthened the position of labor within Mexico's

6.3 Unidentified railroad employee posed at the front of Engine No. 3406. This engine, which ran until 1959, had the distinction of being one of the last steam locomotives to be used on the vast Southern Pacific system. (Courtesy of Donald Duke, Golden West Books, San Marino, California)

social and political infrastructure, while greatly reducing the ability of foreign companies to dictate labor terms to their own workers. The labor law greatly decreased the SP de Mex's ability to control its largest single expense—salaries. It also had the effect of greatly demoralizing company officials. The cooperative effort between the government and the labor unions in forming the Sindicato de Trabajadores Mexicanos also strengthened the barrier against foreign corporate incursions into the country and created an effective hedge against the SP de Mex's ability to regulate labor on the line. After 1939, the SP de Mex was the only significant railroad in the country not under direct Mexican control.

Ironically, the U.S. government also played a role in the railroad's declining fortunes. The restrictive Smoot-Hawley Tariff Act combined with the effects of the Great Depression in the United States to greatly reduce the railroad's ability to rely financially on its parent company, the SP. The United States also appeared more and more reluctant to involve itself too deeply in Mexican financial affairs, pulling the SP de Mex in its receding wake as it backed away from the aggressive involvement in Mexico's finances it had maintained since the Bucareli Agreements. The hemispheric political climate after 1930 did not encourage the kind of aggressive military and corporate penetration that was popular at the turn of the century. The U.S. State Department also became more and more critical of SP de Mex administration after the mid-1930s and increasingly less willing to intercede on the company's behalf.

Third, the SP de Mex contributed to its own downfall. Its desire to cooperate with the increasingly Good Neighbor–oriented U.S. government regarding tax issues, its unwillingness to take advice from its own consultants, and its confusion and misunderstanding over legal issues all caused the railroad's efficiency to slip further and diminished its ability to interact closely and smoothly with the Mexican government. It was not a fall from a terrifying height for the railroad but, instead, a series of hard thumps—none in itself sufficient to kill the company outright but, in total, a punishing set of circumstances.

An undercurrent of ambivalence runs through the SP de Mex's internal correspondence as well as in other parts of the historical record illustrating the railroad's interactions with the government.

This ambivalence and indecisiveness played a significant role in the company's failures because it prevented the company from clearly prioritizing its mission in Mexico. Was it to promote tourism? Was it to serve as a feeder for freight traffic into Mexico? Was it to serve U.S. commercial interests? The railroad tried all of these approaches intermittently after 1930 but never consistently ranked these endeavors by importance or degree of possible success.

General conflicting attitudes held by many North Americans about Mexico may have contributed to this ambivalence. Envy clothed in condescension was often evident. Foreign observers complained that Mexicans were "unbathed and indolent" but were also simultaneously "ignorant of care, untroubled by longing, untortured by ambition, their lot may have more of blessings than we can imagine." Americans remained both dubious and enchanted by Latin American refusal to be molded by modern industrialism—as illustrated by the widely variant attitudes about the Yaquis, for instance. Observers could in one breath describe people in Mexico as "lawless, violent, volatile, and delightful."[57] These conflicting attitudes led to erratic perceptions of Mexican values and attitudes and may have contributed to the railroad's ambivalence and lack of decisiveness about operating in Mexico.

After World War II, finally realizing that Mexico would not allow foreign railroads to wield undue influence over the country's labor conditions, laws, or politics, certainly not in the fashion envisioned by Collis P. Huntington, Edward H. Harriman or Epes Randolph, the SP de Mex shrugged, slumped its shoulders, and relinquished its line to the Mexican government. In the process of acquiring ownership and control of the railroad, Mexico could at last fully manage and regulate the line's operations. The country now had put fully in place a pragmatic set of mechanisms with which to regulate or repulse foreign railroads, as well as developing an underlying ideology to support that ability. José Cantú Corro, a Catholic priest, pointedly expressed Mexican attitudes about foreign encroachment: "Mexico must not be for foreigners; no, a thousand times no . . . Mexico, idolized motherland, nest of affections, mansion of happiness, noble Republic; Mexico, my motherland, let the Saxons never assault your soil, nor implant their false religion, nor tarnish your flag."[58]

CHAPTER 7

Hard Freight

The Impossible as Inevitable

We now return to the primary question posed at the outset: why did the Southern Pacific of Mexico (SP de Mex; Ferrocarril Sud-Pacífico de México) fail? The company had so many assets, skills, and opportunities: the financial and administrative backing of the largest and wealthiest transportation company in the world; a long and chequered history of overcoming difficult technical and logistical problems in the United States; and potentially lucrative markets in both countries for products shipped along the line.

Despite these indicators of success, however, the railroad's failure verged on the inevitable, because it had no way to resolve many of the tensions involved in its relationship with the Mexican government. In the United States, the Southern Pacific Company (SP) had exhibited an extraordinary ability to successfully wrangle agreements and favors from U.S. politicians, landholders, and bankers. But during the railroad's dealings in Mexico, no simple negotiations or agreements could erase widespread and deep-seated Mexican resentment over the loss of territory and sovereignty in the Mexican-American War.

The lessons learned by Mexico stemming from the imbalances between the two countries during the Mexican-American War deeply conditioned the relationship. Mexico was at a disadvantage militarily and economically in the conflict. The war provided the country with an object lesson in the raw inequality of a martial contest with the United States. Decades later, when the railroad arrived, Mexico had every reason to be on guard.

On the other hand, the presence of the SP de Mex provided the country's leaders with an opportunity to focus on non-martial means of maintaining sovereignty. Over the years, law, diplomacy, and negotiation emerged as replacements for military attempts at keeping the United States at bay. These new mechanisms ultimately provided more sophisticated forms of control—and, more importantly, of much greater effectiveness—for the country's leaders than had military force.

The proximity of the two countries also contributed to the tensions between the government and the railroad. The line's sudden appearance in Mexico in 1880 set the tone. What country would not raise its hackles at the new presence of a railroad crossing the border from a country that had only thirty years earlier robbed it of millions of acres of land? The railroad, saturated with nineteenth-century notions of power, progress, and penetration, generated apprehension in Mexico even though the central government had authorized and approved the railroad's coming. "We are in the presence of a great and powerful race that, although friendly, tends to absorb us," warned a Mexico City newspaper upon the railroad's arrival in Sonora.[1]

The importance of the border as a bulwark against U.S. encroachment was also intensified by its distance from central Mexico. The railroad's northern terminus at the border was 1,775 kilometers from Guadalajara. Former president Sebastián Lerdo de Tejada's comment that "between a strong nation and a weak one, the best defense is a desert" referred specifically to the menacing presence of the Sonora Railway and reflected the government's desire to buffer central Mexico from the United States.[2] At the same time, this very distance caused Mexico concern because it made control of the railroad's operations more difficult. Mexican consciousness of the importance and significance of these aspects of the border's proximity and distance remained high during the SP de Mex's tenure in the country and contributed to the country's wariness about the railroad's operations.

The SP, however, did not conceive of the border as a barrier that could hinder its push into Mexico. The dividing line between countries was a kind of reverse mirage for the railroad—it appeared unimportant and insubstantial when in fact it was a very real impediment to its successes. The SP/SP de Mex system ran in an unbroken line from country to country. As soon as it rumbled into the United States at the 31st parallel, the railroad assumed its long-standing U.S. identity as a respected, feared, and profitable line. But heading south, the railroad faced so many new and uncertain elements that it was at constant risk. True, no alchemical transformation occurred when the train crossed over from Nogales, Arizona, into Nogales, Mexico. Not even the name of the town changed. The trains were the same, big Baldwin locomotives capable of pulling cars filled with produce or other goods. The track was the same, capable of rapidly bearing the heaviest loads. And Mexican lands produced no less than those in the United States, issuing forth a cornucopia of potentially lucrative products. But the country also contained obstacles the railroad had not counted upon: the sometimes subtle and increasingly effective forms of control and regulation imposed by the Mexican government.

Had Mexico been the stronger of the two nations, it might well have tried to push its own boundaries northward as eagerly as the United States had pushed to the south, or at least stood its own ground. In contrast, Brazil had maintained its territorial integrity despite being surrounded by ten different countries. If anything, Brazil acted as conqueror of its weaker neighbors, acquiring vast areas of land between 1895 and 1910. Through the efforts of the Baron of Rio-Branco, Brazil acquired 550,000 square kilometers of land during those years—an area larger than France. Mexican leaders, who had overseen their own country's tremendous economic gains during the Porfiriato (1876–1911) expressed admiration of Brazilian territorial expansion: "The development of the vast wealth of Brazil is visible. In almost every case, the progress in these last years has been greater than even the most optimistic had hoped for."[3]

But although Mexico could not gain territory from the United States, it was increasingly unwilling to risk losing even more than it had already surrendered. Although the location of the border in the desert soil had been largely forced upon Mexico and had meant the loss of millions of hectares of land, it nevertheless remained an irrefutable and distinct line after 1853. Within that boundary, Mexico had the absolute right to maintain its own sovereignty, even if it was a right it did not always choose to exercise.

The Mexican-American War experience helped Mexico develop a culture of resistance that manifested itself in the range of ways the country oversaw and regulated the SP de Mex. The SP, on the other hand, had acted historically as an aggressor in U.S. railroading circles, and in dictating many of the actions of its Mexican line, it saw no compelling reason to modify its decades-old attitudes. The example set by the U.S. government's frequent acts of intervention outside of its borders also helped to set an example for the SP (the United States intervened abroad militarily 130 times between 1798 and 1945).[4]

The Mexican Revolution also played a role in Mexican frustration with, and vigilance against, the U.S.'s heavy-handed methods of dealing with the Mexican government. The conflict had brought additional traumas to Mexico as the United States interfered in a variety of ways. From shows of force, such as the bombing of Veracruz, to political pressures, such as the threat of non-recognition by the government of Woodrow Wilson, the United States intensified Mexican dislikes of its northern neighbor and reinvigorated memories of the war that had taken place sixty-five years earlier.

As Mexico's political structure began to resolidify with the start of President Venustiano Carranza's rule, the country wasted no time in increasing the effectiveness of its regulatory mechanisms against U.S. railroads. The United States kept the tensions high between the two countries by rarely giving Mexico an opportunity to let down its guard and by protesting vociferously when it felt its own desires had been denied. When Carranza took over the national lines in 1916, he was met with howls of protest from the numerous foreign stockholders of the National Railways of Mexico (NRM; Ferrocarriles Nacionales de México).

This reaction to the takeover of NRM lines by Carranza's National Constitutional Railroads (NCR; Ferrocarriles Constitucionalistas de México) differed from that which had taken place in Brazil when President Campos Sales had expropriated numerous foreign lines in 1901, or when the Argentines had closely regulated British companies via the Mitre Law of 1907. The Brazilian government's confiscation and purchase of foreign lines did not represent radical nationalism on the part of Sales's government, as it had in Mexico. Rather, Sales acted to alleviate Brazil's financial crisis at the turn of the century rather than to strongly express Brazilian sovereignty in the face of wide-spread British control over the rail system. In fact, British railroad bondholders reacted positively to the expropriations.[5] In Argentina, British firms also approved of the new controls instituted in that country. Although Mexico may have been far closer physically to its railroad investors than Brazil or Argentina, it was much further away from them in terms of consensus or mutuality of purpose.

Why did the SP continue with its efforts in Mexico despite continued losses as well as regular expressions of desire by the line's administrators to stop operations in the country? Again, elements of corporate tradition came into play. The echoes of exhortation by past leaders such as Collis P. Huntington and his successor Edward H. Harriman, and deep-seated notions of conquest, propelled the railroad forward. These roots ran deep. "We have bought not only a railroad, but an empire," noted Harriman in 1901 upon taking over the railroad from Huntington.[6]

The difficulties the railroad faced in completing the gap between Tepic and La Quemada added heat to the bonfire. The railroad pushed on with the same determination it had shown in completing the difficult U.S. transcontinental line, bolstered by writings in the U.S. press about the value the completion would provide. But while the railroad's administrators could understand geographic challenges, they were hard-pressed to grasp the more subtle cultural and interpersonal requirements of successfully doing business in Mexico.

The SP reaped income of $120 million U.S. in the United States in 1909, the year of the SP de Mex's incorporation—an amount equal to nearly half of Mexico's entire federal budget that year.[7] But despite the potential clout and power such income implied, and although it occasionally expressed a desire to remake Mexico in the image of its profitable U.S. territory, the SP could not wield economic, political, or legal domination over the west coast of Mexico in any meaningful way.

The parent SP's successes in its homeland were even more striking when contrasted with the legal, financial, and technical struggles of its Mexican line. In 1926, as the SP de Mex struggled to complete the span across the Salsipuedes Gorge, the SP achieved status as the second-largest company in the United States, with total assets of more than $2 billion U.S.[8] But all of that wealth and experience could not translate into success for the SP de Mex. Mexico, like the oyster enclosing the grain of sand, ultimately absorbed the railroad completely and turned it into a pearl for its own intranational uses. U.S. railroad executives desired Mexico as a new frontier, but in the end, the railroad became a kind of frontier for Mexico: a chance to build and maintain its own sovereignty.

NOTES

Chapter 1

1. "R. R. Head Sees a Silver Lining," *Arizona Daily Star*, June 25, 1938.
2. Nicoli, *El estado de Sonora*, 10.
3. Talbot, *Railway Conquest*, 12.
4. Raat, "Positivism in Díaz Mexico," 67.

Chapter 2

1. Several major gaps remain unfilled in Mexican railroad scholarship. Although considerable recent scholarship exists—notably the work of Sandra Kuntz Ficker and Paolo Riguzzi—there is no up-to-date overarching, synthetic history of Mexican railroads.

The National Railways of Mexico (NRM; Ferrocarriles Nacionales de México) also played a vital role in creating a national transportation structure, building Mexican pride and providing labor for thousands of workers. Yet the closest thing to a comprehensive history of the NRM was written just after World War II.

Mexican railroad labor also still needs a new synthetic analysis, although considerable work has been done on that topic. Most studies take a narrow approach. They include Antonio Alonso's *El movimiento ferrocarrilero en México, 1958–1959: De la conciliación a la lucha de clases* (Mexico City: Ediciones Era, 1972); and Luciano Cedillo's *Vaaamonos: [sic] Luchas, anecdotas y problemas de los ferrocarrileros* (Mexico City: Ediciones de Cultura Popular, 1979).

2. The Panama Railway (constructed 1855) did pass through a U.S. possession—the Canal Zone—after 1903. On the question of Panamanian sovereignty over the railroad, see E. J. Castillero's *El ferrocarril de Panama y su*

historia (Panama: Imprenta Nacional, 1932). For a contemporary view of the railroad's early presence in the zone and detailed statistics on the line's international shipments, see Joseph L. Bristow's *Report of Joseph L. Bristow, Special Panama Railroad Commissioner, to the Secretary of War, June 24, 1905* (Washington, D.C.: Office of Administration, Isthmian Canal Affairs, 1905).

3. Coatsworth, *Growth Against Development*, 35–36. The history of this first line has received extensive attention. Baz and Gallo wrote an excellent study of the line in 1874, the year after its completion: *Historia del Ferrocarril Mexicano*.

4. Randall, "Mexico's Pre-Revolutionary Reckoning with Railroads," 15.

5. McNeely, *Railways of Mexico*, 6.

6. Probing studies of this line have included Mancera's *Ferrocarril interoceánico*; Glick's *Straddling the Isthmus of Tehuantepec*; and J. Fred Rippy's "Diplomacy of the United States and Mexico Regarding the Isthmus of Tehuantepec," *Mississippi Valley Historical Review*, 6, no. 4 (March 1920): 503–531. Useful primary sources include U.S. State Department consular reports from 1930–1939 (Decimal File 812, 1370/161, National Archives and Records Administration), with comprehensive discussions about the value of the railroad and its final transfer back to the Mexican government in 1937, many years after its initial appropriation by the United States through the Gadsden Purchase.

7. Randall, "Mexico's Pre-Revolutionary Reckoning with Railroads," 6.

8. Raat, "Positivism in Díaz Mexico," 72–73.

9. McNeely, *Railways of Mexico*, 7.

10. Bethell, *Mexico since Independence*, 71–74.

11. For an outstanding look at the MCR during the Porfiriato and González' interregnum, see Ficker's work, including "Economic Backwardness and Firm Strategy," as well as her 1995 book on the MCR, *Empresa extranjera y mercado interno*. The SP de Mex and the MCR were both American-organized lines with early ties to, and influences originating from, the Atcheson, Topeka & Santa Fe. A number of parallels exist between the two lines, including their transition from being tightly bound to their parent company to more freestanding operations in Mexico; huge investments by their respective parent companies in the United States; and some similar failures in adapting to business in Mexico.

12. Alzati, *Historia de la Mexicanización de los Ferrocarriles*, 35.

13. Limantour, quoted in "Fascinación e importancia de los ferrocarriles en México," by Sergio Ortiz Hernán, in *Los ferrocarrileros hablan*, 33.

14. José Yves Limantour and Alberto J. Pani, Carranza's director of railroads, each deserve detailed study and analysis. Yet Díaz Dufoo's biography of Limantour is now nearly a century old, and Pani has not been subjected to close scrutiny in many years. Ezequiel Adeodato Chávez wrote a study during

the revolution entitled *Notas acerca del estudio del ingeniero D. Alberto J. Pani, subsecretario de instrucción pública y bellas artes sobre "La instrucción rudimentaria en la república"* (Mexico: n.p., 1912), while Pani himself penned a two-volume autobiography in 1950 (*Apuntes autobiográficos* [Mexico City: M. Porrúa, 1950]). Writings on Limantour also appear to be scarce, being limited to Dufoo's biography, several pamphlets published on him during the revolution, and a handful of books discussing a nineteenth-century court case between his father by the same name and the city of San Francisco.

15. McNeely, *Railways of Mexico*, 16.

16. Bethell, *Mexico since Independence*, 114–115.

17. Caballero, *Evolución de la frontera norte*, 90.

18. Schivelbusch, *Railway Journey*, 37.

19. Macedo, *Evolución mercantil*, 223, as quoted in Powell, *Railroads of Mexico*, 189.

20. *Washington Post*, November 11, 1908.

21. Raat, "Positivism in Díaz Mexico," 213–214.

22. Roa, *El problema ferrocarrilero*, 26–28.

23. Pletcher, *Rails, Mines and Progress*, 21–23.

24. Macedo, *Evolución mercantil*, 205, as noted in Pletcher, *Rails, Mines and Progress*, 25.

25. Early government publications on railroad legislation include the useful *Reseña sobre los principales ferrocarriles construidos en México* (Mexico City: SCOP, 1892). The introduction by Ing. Luis E. Bracamontes, the secretary of public works (secretario de obras públicas), shows some of the SCOP's priorities. He notes that, among other routes, a link from Mexico City to Sonora was "intuitively" the first priority for Mexico and expresses his desire for a trans-isthmian line. However, Mexico would not reach its west coast by rail until the SP de Mex completed its line in 1927. The SCOP also published other detailed works during the Porfiriato, including *Reglamento general de ferrocarriles* (Mexico City: SCOP, 1894) and *Reglamento para la construcción, conservación y servicio de los ferrocarriles* (Mexico City: SCOP, 1895).

26. Díaz to Albert K. Owen, May 2, 1896, Albert K. Owen Collection, Huntington Library.

27. Pletcher, *Rails, Mines and Progress*, 313.

28. Coatsworth, *Growth Against Development*, 38.

29. Macedo, *Evolución mercantil*, 207.

30. Kolko, *Railroads and Regulation*, 57–63.

31. Bernardo Reyes to José Maria Maytorena, November 4, 1909, José Maria Maytorena Collection, Honnold Library, Claremont Colleges. Hereafter MCHL.

32. Maytorena to Rodolfo Reyes, April 10, 1909. MCHL.

33. Cuellar, *La situación financiera*, 89–90.

34. Roa, *El problema ferrocarrilero*, 116.

35. Powell, *Railroads of Mexico*, 4–6.

36. The first widely published government publication detailing the laws of the NRM was *Estatuos; Ferrocarriles Nacionales de México; Ley, decreto y escritura relativos a la constitución de la compañía.*

37. Gurza, *La política ferrocarrilera del gobierno*, 116, as noted in Frederick C. Turner, *The Dynamic of Mexican Nationalism* (Chapel Hill: University of North Carolina, 1970).

38. Price, Waterhouse & Co., *National Railways of Mexico*, 6.

39. James W. Wilkie, *The Mexican Revolution: Federal Expenditure and Social Change since 1910* (Berkeley: University of California Press, 1970): 28, 144–145, 293.

40. *Second Annual Report of Ferrocarriles Nacionales de México, for the Fiscal Year Ended June 30, 1910.* All monies noted in these NRM annual reports (and elsewhere herein unless otherwise noted) are in Mexican pesos.

41. *Fourth Annual Report of Ferrocarriles Nacionales de México, for the Fiscal Year Ended June 30, 1912*, 14.

42. *Sixth Annual Report of Ferrocarriles Nacionales de México, for the Fiscal Year Ended June 30, 1914*, 15.

43. Ibid. Also see U.S. State Department discussions about the Carrancista takeover of the NRM in a September 21, 1916 memorandum, "Records of the Department of State Relating to the Internal Affairs of Mexico, 1910–1929," Roll 236, 812.74–812.77/109, National Archives and Records Administration. Hereafter NARA.

44. Memorandum #3 from Alberto J. Pani, November 17, 1916, FA Box 109 (17), National Railways of Mexico, Fall Collection, Huntington Library. Copies of the same memos are also contained in State Department consular reports, ibid.

45. McNeely, *Railways of Mexico*, 30.

46. "Department of State Consular Reports for Mexico, 1910–1929," N274, Roll 237, 311 ff., NARA.

47. Estimates of destruction or damage of railroad property during the revolution vary greatly. Powell estimates that about half of Mexico's 10,000 boxcars were in need of replacement by 1920 (*Railroads of Mexico*, 43). Camín and Meyer note losses of about a third: 3,873 railroad cars, and a surprisingly low estimate of 50 locomotives destroyed (*In the Shadow of the Mexican Revolution*, 71).

48. Memorandum #3 from Alberto J. Pani, November 17, 1916, FA Box 109 (17), National Railways of Mexico, Fall Collection, Huntington Library.

49. Ibid.

50. Memorandum #4 from Alberto J. Pani, "Department of State Consular Reports for Mexico, 1910–1929," N274, Roll 236, NARA.

51. Authors pondering this question around the 1914–1915 period included Loría, *Lo que ha sido y debe de ser la política ferrocarrilera*, and Roa, *El problema ferrocarrilero*.

52. Roa, *El problema ferrocarrilero*, 271.

53. McNeely, *Railways of Mexico*, 33. Camín and Meyer (*In the Shadow of the Mexican Revolution*, 80–84) also have a succinct and clear discussion of the role of the ICB in helping Obregón gain a toehold for U.S. recognition prior to the Bucareli Agreements of 1923.

54. Macedo, *Evolución mercantil*, 223, as quoted in Powell, *The Railroads of Mexico*, 189.

55. Font, *El desastre de los Ferrocarriles Nacionales de México*, 12–13.

56. Roa, *El problema ferrocarrilero*, 40.

Chapter 3

1. McNeely, *Railways of Mexico*, 39.

2. Kirchner and Signor, *Southern Pacific of Mexico and the West Coast Route*, 13. This is the only book written on the SP de Mex. While it contains no analytical material, it is full of factual information about the line, primarily pertaining to routes, specific types of trains, etc. Three useful but very dated review articles on the railroad also exist: Hardy, "El Ferrocarril Sud-Pacífico"; Wyllys, "Sud-Pacifico: Postscript on a Railroad"; and Trennert, "Southern Pacific of Mexico." The most recent scholarly article, "Twenty Years to Nogales: The Building of the Guaymas-Nogales Railroad," by Boyd, which studies the Sonora Railway before it evolved into the SP de Mex, is riddled with factual errors and should be used cautiously. No Mexican works have been written about the railroad.

3. Waters, *Steel Trails to Santa Fe*, 61.

4. Ibid.

5. "Department of State Consular Reports for Nogales, 1881–1910," National Archives and Records Administration. Hereafter NARA.

6. Nicoli, *El estado de Sonora*, 13.

7. "Compañia Limitada del Ferrocarril de Sonora. Tarifa de distancia de carga, Numero 1C. Rige por la clasificación impresa, adjunta, y por las reglas de la tarifa No. 1B." Mexico City: SCOP, 1995.

8. Trennert, "Southern Pacific of Mexico," 266.

9. Box 2, Huntington Library, SP de Mex Collection [uncataloged]. Hereafter HLSPM.

10. A good discussion of Díaz' desires for military control of various regions in Mexico can be found in the anthology *Porfirio Díaz frente al descontento popular regional* (Friedrich Katz, ed.; Mexico City: Universidad Iberoamericana, 1986).

11. Hardy, "The Revolution and the Railroads of Mexico," 249.

12. "S.P. Plans Line to Mexico City," *San Francisco Examiner*, February 17, 1923.

13. Frank A. Vanderlip, "From Farm Boy to Financier: Stories of Railroad Moguls," *Saturday Evening Post*, February 9, 1935 [date is clipped off original kept by the Arizona Historical Society].

14. Julius Kruttschnitt, "Notes and Memoranda," typescript, March 19, 1913, Item 1, Box 4, HLSPM.

15. Ministero de Comunicaciones y Obras Publicas, *Cuadros estadísticos de ferrocarriles* (Mexico City: Talleres Graficos de la Secretaria de Comunicaciones y Obras Publicas, 1912), 14–15, 26.

16. G. González to SCOP, July 14, 1910. Report entitled "Ferrocarril de Sonora, Compañía del Ferrocarril Sud Pacífico de México," Archivo General de la Nación, Secretaría de Comunicaciones y Obras Públicas (SCOP) Collection. Hereafter SCOP.

17. Collis P. Huntington, "The Nicaragua Canal: Would it Pay the United States to Construct It?" Text of a speech to the Galveston, Texas, Chamber of Commerce, March 16, 1900, Rare Book Collection, Huntington Library.

18. News clipping, unidentified [ca. 1917], Special Collections, University of Arizona, Tucson.

19. Southern Pacific 1911 annual report.

20. Cooper, "Arizona Border Towns and the Huerta Revolution."

21. Southern Pacific 1914 annual report, 23.

22. Memoradum #1 from Carranza, December 4, 1914, FA Box 109 (17), National Railways of Mexico, Fall Collection, Huntington Library.

23. Inspector E. Coretta to Vicente Octoy, head of SCOP, November 11, 1916, SCOP.

24. Ibid.

25. Octoy to Coretta, December 17, 1916, SCOP.

26. Coretta to Octoy, November 8, 1916, SCOP.

27. See, for example, the voluminous series of papers in SCOP entitled "Inspección technica de ferrocarriles, Zona VI." The government's internal reports on the SP de Mex can be generally found throughout Record Group 171 of the Fomento de Ferrocarriles, SCOP, in the Archivo General de la Nación.

28. Randolph to Julius Kruttschnitt, July 9, 1913, HLSPM.

29. See, for example, the lengthy list of costs incurred by the railroad, as noted by the NRM's two chief inspectors, R. D. Micotti and Félix L. Trigos, in a report to Frederico Torres, Presidente de la Comisión Revisora de Reclamaciones del Ferrocarril Sud-Pacífico de México, February 3, 1921, SCOP.

30. Box 28, HLSPM.

31. File on Reclamaciones, SCOP.

32. Box 16, HLSPM.

33. E. R. Jones to Titcomb, Dec. 30, 1922, HLSPM.

34. Titcomb to Kruttschnitt, Oct. 11, 1921, HLSPM.

35. Titcomb to Kruttschnitt, May 6, 1922, HLSPM.

36. Alvaro Obregón to George Jackson, SP de Mex representative in Mexico City, May 31, 1922, HLSPM. Also see NARA consular report from Guaymas consulate to Department of State, Nov. 21, 1924, for a discussion of Obregón's land holdings in Navojoa and the tie to railroad operations.

37. Box 17, HLSPM.

38. Harvey B. Titcomb to Julius Kruttschnitt, May 6, 1922, HLSPM.

39. Titcomb to Kruttschnitt, November 13, 1922, HLSPM.

40. Box 17, HLSPM.

41. Kruttschnitt to Titcomb, November 9, 1922, HLSPM.

42. "Memorandum of Agreement Entered into between Mr. Alvaro Obregón, President of the Republic, Representing the Federal Government, Hereinafter called 'The Government,' and Mr. H. B. Titcomb, President of the Southern Pacific Railroad Company of Mexico, Hereinafter Called 'The Company,'" March 2, 1923, HLSPM.

43. *Diario Oficial*, January 16 and 22, 1923.

44. Accurate figures of the total amount expended by the railroad on their Mexican operations by the end of the revolution are difficult to come by and vary greatly. This figure appeared in the SP's own 1922 annual report. However, the *Boston News Bureau*, April 22, 1922, in a story entitled "Southern Pacific's Mexican Investment," noted that the company had invested $122,027,733 U.S. to that point.

45. "Southern Pacific's Mexican Investment," *Boston News Bureau*, April 22, 1922. The SP de Mex would later issue a brief internal paper in August 1948 entitled "Oil Prospects on the West Coast," which detailed oil explorations they and others had undertaken in Mexico, but with poor results. They concluded, "Up to the present time, apparently oil men have concluded that there are no substantial oil deposits on the West Coast."

46. "Southern Pacific to Build Mexican Road," *New York Herald*, March 3, 1923.

47. Titcomb to Julius Kruttschnitt, March 2, 1923, Box 16, HLSPM.

48. Southern Pacific 1922 annual report.

49. Notes accompanying text of construction resumption speeches, HLSPM.

50. *Excélsior*, March 11, 1923.

51. "Phoenix to Mexico City Rail Line Is in Prospect," *Arizona Republican*, April 14, 1922.

52. Deverell, *Railroad Crossing*, 34–60.

53. Ibid., 34.

Chapter 4

1. "Mexico to See New Railroad Opened Shortly," *New York Herald Tribune*, December 8, 1926.

2. Yenne, *History of the Southern Pacific*, 27.

3. Kirchner and Signor, *Southern Pacific of Mexico and the West Coast Route*, 47.

4. Ibid., 43.

5. SCOP Technical Reports for 1925 and 1926; also detailed in Kirchner and Signor, *Southern Pacific of Mexico and the West Coast Route*, 49.

6. M. Cabrera, director of railways, to the head of SCOP, February 27, 1924, Archivo General de la Nación, Secretaría de Comunicaciones y Obras Públicas (SCOP) Collection. Hereafter SCOP.

7. Cabrera to Harvey B. Titcomb, Item 1, Box 23, Huntington Library, SP de Mex Collection [uncataloged]. Hereafter HLSPM.

8. Ciphered telegram from Harvey B. Titcomb to Julius Kruttschnitt, July 25, 1924, "Some extremely embarrassing circumstances mitigating against us," warned Titcomb, Item 1, Box 23, HLSPM.

9. M. Cabrera to the head of SCOP, February 27, 1924, SCOP.

10. A number of disparate sources disagree on the length of this final Tepic–La Quemada section, ranging from Donovan Hofsommer's 1986 history of the SP, *Southern Pacific, 1901–1985*, which inaccurately notes the section's completed length as being 90 miles, to an extremely specific 102.816 miles, as noted in company records from a survey in the 1920s. Earlier estimates had put the line's length at 102.79 miles; later ones at about 105 miles; others had rounded it down to 102 miles. The probable reason for these differing lengths was that earlier surveys assumed certain curvatures of track; sharper curves meant longer distances and thus higher construction costs, but the exigencies of proper construction meant that changes in track curvature during actual construction were unavoidable. The final section of track as completed in 1927 was probably very close to 102 miles.

11. Item 3, Box X, HLSPM, contains detailed accountings of the bidding for the construction work.

12. "Engineers Club Has Own Celebration of Completion of Road," *Tucson Daily Citizen*, April 20, 1927.

13. Technical Inspector C. Molina to SCOP, July 27, 1925, SCOP.

14. Technical Inspector Rafael Luna to L. M. Rose, Sinaloa Division Superintendent, October 16, 1926, SCOP.

15. Inspector C. Molina to director of SCOP, February 14, 1926, SCOP.

16. Inspector Luna to Rose, SCOP.

17. Martín Elizondo to Interim Director of SCOP, December 11, 1926; and Director's response to Elizondo, December 21, 1926, SCOP.

18. "Construction of Line Tepic to La Quemada." September 3, 1925 to August 4, 1926, File No. 300.4, Part 1, Box I, HLSPM.

19. Ibid.

20. File No. 300.4, Part 1, Box 1, HLSPM.

21. "Mexico to See New Railroad Opened Shortly," *New York Herald Tribune*, December 8, 1926.

22. "Espee Building Mexican Lines," *Los Angeles Times*, November 10, 1923, II-6.

23. Sproule to McDonald and deForest to Sproule, April 1927, Box 18, HLSPM.

24. Shoup to Chandler, April 21, 1927, HLSPM.

25. "S.P. Sends First Coast Train Into Guadalajara," *San Francisco Chronicle*, May 14, 1927.

26. Titcomb to Sproule, April 21, 1927, HLSPM.

27. "Resolutions Adopted by the Board of Directors of the Southern Pacific Railroad Co. of Mexico Relative to Concessions and Construction of Line," n.d., HLSPM.

28. *Tucson Citizen*, April 17, 1927.

29. See, for example, the 1927 report the SP de Mex presented to the secretary of communications and public works, *Informe anual de la Compañía del Ferrocarril Sud-Pacífico de México por el año terminado el 31 de Diciembre 1927.*

30. Sproule to Titcomb, December 21, 1927, Box 18, HLSPM.

31. Sproule to Titcomb, December 31, 1926, Box 1, HLSPM.

32. U.S. consular reports, 1910–1919, November 23, 1928, N274, Roll 237, National Archives and Records Administration.

33. Shoup to Titcomb, June 24, 1927, Item 3, Box 22, HLSPM.

34. "130 Tucsonians Leave Wednesday to Reside at Guadalajara, Mex.," *Arizona Citizen*, July 25, 1927.

35. "Moving SPdeM Offices into Mexico," File No. 354.101, Part I, Item 3, Box 22, HLSPM.

36. In addition to the other Mexican officials cited in this chapter, Inspector J. Encarnación Sahagún, in a series of communications to Rafael Sandoval, Chief of Railroads at SCOP, September 23 and October 3, 1929, also discusses a number of these issues, as does an unnamed SCOP official on May 8, 1929, to the director of SCOP, SCOP.

37. Jesus A. Cruz to Rafael Sandoval, November 23, 1927, SCOP.

38. Technical Inspector Alberto Crespo to the head of SCOP, September 24, 1929, SCOP.

39. From various internal SP de Mex sources; rounded figures for SP de Mex net profits can be found in Hardy's "El Ferrocarril Sud-Pacífico." Some of Hardy's figures are rounded incorrectly. See Appendix for detailed financial data on the company.

40. Technical Inspector O. Dara to the head of SCOP, October 5, 1929, SCOP.

41. Inspector de Primera de Ferrocarriles [signature illegible] to J. A. Small, SP de Mex, December 5, 1928, SCOP.

42. SCOP Interim Subsecretary J. J. Ostos to Sloan, October 3, 1929, SCOP.

43. Earl B. Sloan, who headed up the company's large railroad engineering department, remained nearly invisible and rarely surfaces in correspondence or discussion, but this brief descriptive line about him came from an article in the *Arizona Daily Star*, April 22, 1927. Sloan eventually became a vice president in the organization late in the SP de Mex's life.

44. Sr. Sandoval, chief of railroads for SCOP, June 23 and 29, 1928, to Sloan, SCOP.

45. "Claim Against Mexican Government for Damages in Revolution in 1929. 10 Percent Gross Tax Settlement," File 900-2, Section 6, HLSPM.

46. Titcomb to Shoup, July 9, 1932, detailing the events of 1929, Item 3, Box 2, HLSPM.

47. Sproule to McDonald, January 6, 1928, HLSPM.

48. Shoup to deForest, November 23, 1928, Box 18, HLSPM.

49. Dwight Morrow to Paul Shoup, July 15, 1929, Box 15, HLSPM.

50. Shoup to Holden, June 5, 1929, Box 19, HLSPM.

51. Knight, *U.S.–Mexican Relations*, 81, 88.

52. Hall, *Oil, Banks and Politics*, 6–7.

53. Brown, *Oil and Revolution in Mexico*, 126.

54. Hall, *Oil, Banks and Politics*, 35.

55. "E. H. Harriman's Dream of Railway Development," noted in the *Boston News Bureau*, April 22, 1922; "Randolph's Great Dream Comes True," *Tucson Citizen*, March 11, 1923; "Dream of E. H. Harriman Nears Completion," *New York Commercial*, July 17, 1924; "One of Harriman's Dreams a Reality in Mexico," *Kansas City Star*, January 11, 1925; "Rail Dream of Epes Randolph Unites Mexico," *Arizona Daily Star*, Spring 1927 (clipping from Arizona Historical Society, n.d.).

56. Hofsommer, *Southern Pacific, 1901–1985*, 116–117.

Chapter 5

1. Benjamin and Wasserman, *Provinces of the Revolution*, 20.

2. Palacio quoted in article by Cott, "Mexican Diplomacy and the Chinese Issue," 64.

3. Ibid., 78.

4. Ibid., 78.

5. Alan Knight, "Racism, Revolution, and *Indigenismo*: Mexico, 1910–1940," in *The Idea of Race in Latin America, 1870–1940* (Richard Graham, ed.; Austin, TX: University of Austin Press, 1990), 96.

6. Price, Waterhouse & Co., *National Railways of Mexico*, 368–369.

7. See discussions between General Cándido Aguilar, secretary of foreign relations under Carranza, and a variety of civil servants including R. P. Negri (the Mexican consulate in San Francisco) and Herminio Perez Abreu (general director of consulates in Mexico City), July 1916, File No. IV-262-16, Archivo Histórico de la Secretaría de Relaciones Exteriores.

8. Tijerina to SCOP, July 25 and 29, 1930, Archivo General de la Nación, Secretaría de Comunicaciones y Obras Públicas (SCOP) Collection. Hereafter SCOP.

9. "Manifesto sobre el porqué de la existencia y actividades del comité anti-Chino," April 1924, Archivo General de la Nación, Fondo Obregón-Calles, 104-ch-16.

10. González and Lara, *Chinos y antichinos en México*, 97.

11. Hu-Dehart, "Development and Rural Rebellion," 74.

12. "Plucky Railway Attorney Puts Yaquís to Flight," n.p., June 4, 1908, Frederick Starr Papers, UCLA, Special Collections. Hereafter Starr Papers, UCLA.

13. Spicer, *Yaquis*, 237.

14. "Department of State Consular Reports for Mexico, 1910–1929," April 24, 1923, N274, Roll 237, National Archives and Records Administration. Hereafter NARA.

15. Harvey B. Titcomb to Julius Kruttschnitt, February 1, 1924, Huntington Library, SP de Mex Collection [uncataloged]. Hereafter HLSPM.

16. Gonzales, "U.S. Copper Companies, the Mine Workers' Movement, and the Mexican Revolution, 1910–1920," 528.

17. Kirchner and Signor, *Southern Pacific of Mexico and the West Coast Route*, 33.

18. Mishima, *Seite migraciones japonesas en México*, 184.

19. News clippings, n.p., n.d., Starr Papers, UCLA.

20. *Mexican Herald*, 1906 [n.d.], Box 7, Starr Papers, UCLA.

21. *Chihuahua Enterprise*, n.p., n.d., Starr Papers, UCLA.

22. Thomas, *Uncertain Sanctuary*, 18.

23. Anchondo to Aguirre, May 28, 1923, Archivo Histórico de la Secretaría de Relaciones Exteriores. Hereafter AHSRE.

24. Ortiz, subsecretary of foreign relations, to J.E. Anchondo, July 17, 1923, AHSRE.

25. Martin, *Representative Modern Constitutions*, 180.

26. Bailey, *¡Viva Cristo Rey!*, Chapter 3, "Of Men and Laws."

27. Meyer, *Cristero Rebellion*, 85.

28. Consular reports, 1910–1919, January 3, 1928, N274, Roll 237, NARA.

29. McDonald to Holden, Box 19, HLSPM.

30. Sproule to Titcomb, September 17, 1926, HLSPM.

31. Bethell, *Mexico since Independence*, 214.

32. Meyer, *Cristero Rebellion*, 83–84.

33. Bernstein, *Foreign Investment in Latin America*, 67.

34. Waters, *Steel Trails to Santa Fe*, 62.

35. Kirchner and Signor, *Southern Pacific of Mexico and the West Coast Route*, 72.

36. Ibid., 53.

37. Moncada, *Me llamo Empalme*, 30.

38. Kirchner and Signor, *Southern Pacific of Mexico and the West Coast Route*, 34.

39. Moncada, *Me llamo Empalme*, 42.

40. Randall Clark, ed., *Dictionary of Literary Biography*, Vol. 44 (Detroit: Gale Research Co., 1986), 74.

41. Moncada, *Me llamo Empalme*, 49.

42. Price, Waterhouse & Co., *National Railways of Mexico*, 12–40.

43. Kirchner and Signor, *Southern Pacific of Mexico and the West Coast Route*, 21.

Chapter 6

1. Anderson, *Outcasts in their Own Land*, 324.

2. "Sáenz Outlines Labor Law Aims," *Excélsior*, July 11, 1931.

3. Ibid.

4. "Sáenz Outlines Labor Law Aims," *Excélsior*, July 11, 1931.

5. "Mexican Labor Law of 1931," From May 29, 1931 to Dec. 28, 1933, File No. SPM 013-2, Section 2, Item 1, Box 10, Huntington Library, SP de Mex Collection [uncataloged]. Hereafter HLSPM.

6. Titcomb to Shoup, May 29, 1931, Item 1, Box 10, HLSPM.

7. Shoup to Holden, July 11, 1931, Item 1, Box 10, HLSPM.

8. File SPM 013-2, Section 2, Item 1, Box 10, HLSPM. See in particular the letter from Titcomb to Shoup, September 18, 1931.

9. Harvey B. Titcomb to Paul Shoup, September 18, 1931, Box 10, HLSPM.

10. Shoup to Holden, September 24, 1931, Box 10, HLSPM.

11. Hale Holden to Paul Shoup, September 24, 1931, Box 10, HLSPM.

12. "Records of the Department of State Relating to the Internal Affairs of Mexico, 1930–39," 812.76/180–812.77/1290, National Archives and Records Administration. Hereafter NARA.

13. Sáenz to E. B. Sloan, October 5, 1931, Box 10, HLSPM.

14. Six workers, signatures illegible, to J. A. Small, October 12, 1931, Item 1, Box 10, HLSPM.

15. Item 1, Box 10, HLSPM.

16. File No. SPM 210-002, Part 1, Item 1, Box 7, HLSPM.

17. "Added Changes Face S.P. de M.," *Arizona Daily Star*, June 2, 1932; other sources in HLSPM (primarily Box 10).

18. Hardy, "El Ferrocarril Sud-Pacífico," 265.

19. E. W. Eaton, vice-consul, Mazatlán, to U.S. secretary of state, July 26, 1932, Decimal File 812, NARA.

20. *Excélsior*, December 4, 1932.

21. Kirchner and Signor, *Southern Pacific of Mexico and the West Coast Route*, 96.

22. Douglas to Hale Holden, July 26, 1933, Item 6, Box 14, HLSPM.

23. Zimmerman, *Los pactos obreros*, 59–67.

24. Bailey, *¡Viva Cristo Rey!*, 48.

25. Holden to Walter Douglas, November 27, 1933, Item 1, Box 10, HLSPM.

26. Kirchner and Signor, *Southern Pacific of Mexico and the West Coast Route*, 40–41.

27. Brown, "Foreign and Native-Born Workers in Porfirian Mexico," 800.

28. Douglas to MacDonald, March 30, 1938, Box 7, HLSPM.

29. Brown, "Foreign and Native-Born Workers in Porfirian Mexico," 817.

30. *Diario Oficial*, January 16 and 22, 1923.

31. Hugh Neill to Paul Shoup, December 9, 1930, HLSPM.

32. File No. 310-973, Part 9, Item 5, Box 28, HLSPM.

33. Clarke to Stimson, October 18, 1931, Decimal File 812, NARA.

34. "Claim of Mexican Government for Duties, Fines, and Penalties for Fuel Oil Taken by SPdeM Locomotives Across Border Without Being Manifested in Customhouse." SPM 023-6, Section 1, Item 1, Box 22, HLSPM.

35. As quoted in the railroad's "Brief Outline of the More Important Current Affairs of the Southern Pacific Railroad Company of Mexico," Box 10, HLSPM.

36. "History–Southern Pacific Railroad Company of Mexico (MJW-275)." File No. SPdeM 110-3 (History), Part I, Item 1, Box 8, HLSPM.

37. Item 1C, Box I, HLSPM.

38. Box 7, HLSPM.

39. All brochures and articles cited are from the private collection of ephemera, Donald Duke, publisher of Golden West Books, San Marino, California. Also, *Sunset Magazine*, 1936–1941. Coincidentally, SP de Mex official Paul Shoup was the man responsible for starting *Sunset Magazine* in 1898. He began the publication as a hobby while clerking for the SP as a young man at the station in San Bernardino, California. A talented writer, Shoup published poems and short stories in a variety of publications.

40. Hilton to Mercier, June 7, 1945, Item 3, Box 20, HLSPM.

41. Medina to Summerlin [translated], "Department of State Consular Reports for Mexico, 1910–1929," N274, Roll 238, December 26, 1919, NARA.

42. Titcomb to Paul Shoup, September 29, 1931, Box 1, HLSPM.

43. Walter Thomas to Hale Holden, April 23, 1934, Box 1, HLSPM.

44. File No. SPM 120, Section 1, HLSPM.

45. Kirchner and Signor, *Southern Pacific of Mexico and the West Coast Route*, 98.

46. See, for example, "1937 Net Income of S.P. Lines Drops 94.78 percent; Annual Report Reflects Heavy Expenses and Low Earnings," *Southern Pacific Bulletin* (April 1938), 9.

47. "Los Ferrocarriles Nacionales van a ser administrados por los trabajadores," *El Universal*, June 26, 1937.

48. *Diario Oficial*, April 30, 1938.

49. For instance, "La nacionalización de los ferrocarriles," *El Universal*, June 25, 1937.

50. Maurice Cowen to James Roosevelt, assistant to the president, July 26, 1937, Decimal File 812, NARA.

51. A. F. Yepis, Guaymas vice-consul, to Secretary of State Cordell Hull, March 9, 1938, Decimal File 812, NARA.

52. Yepis to Hull, April 25, 1938, Decimal File 812, NARA.

53. Calculated from a series of internal sources listing annual losses. HLSPM.

54. *La Gaceta*, June 30, 1938.

55. Font, *El desastre de los Ferrocarriles Nacionales de México*, 43–50.

56. Kirchner and Signor, *Southern Pacific of Mexico and the West Coast Route*, 101–102.

57. Pike, *United States and Latin America*, 86–87.

58. Smith, *Talons of the Eagle*, 107.

Chapter 7

1. "Quien vencerá siempre es el progreso," *La Constitución*, June 4, 1881, as cited in Miguel Tinker Salas, *In the Shadow of the Eagles: Sonora and the Transformation of the Border during the Porfiriato* (Berkeley: University of California Press, 1997), 88.

2. Pletcher, "The Development of Railroads in Sonora," 15.

3. Burns, *History of Brazil*, 320, quoting the Mexican chargé d'affaires in Rio de Janeiro to the secretary of foreign relations, May 5, 1910, Folder No. 3053-2, Archivo de la Secretaría de Relaciones Exteriores del [*sic*] México.

4. James Chace, "America Knows Best," *Los Angeles Times Book Review*, May 4, 1997, 9.

5. Topik, *Political Economy of the Brazilian State*, 97.

6. Hofsommer, *Southern Pacific, 1901–1985*, 9.

7. James W. Wilkie, *The Mexican Revolution: Federal Expenditure and Social Change since 1910* (Berkeley: University of California Press, 1970), 22; Hofsommer, *Southern Pacific, 1901–1985*, 50.

8. Hofsommer, *Southern Pacific, 1901–1985*, 116.

BIBLIOGRAPHY

Primary Sources

AGN   Archivo General de la Nación, Mexico City, Mexico. All items from Record Group 288 of the Secretaría de Comunicaciones y Obras Públicas [Fondo SCOP, Serie Ferrocarriles, Expediente 288/X–X], Galeria 5].

AHSRE   Archivo Histórico de la Secretaría de Relaciones Exteriores, Mexico City, Mexico.

ARE   Archivo de las Relaciones Extranjeros, Mexico City, Mexico.

DRFR   Doheny Research Foundation Records, Special Collections, Occidental College, Los Angeles, CA.

HLSPM   Southern Pacific of Mexico Collection, Huntington Library, San Marino, CA.

MCHL   José Maria Maytorena Collection, Honnold Library, Claremont Colleges, Claremont, CA.

NARA   Consular Reports to Mexico, National Archives and Records Administration, Washington, D.C.

Starr Papers   Frederick Starr Papers, Special Collections, University of California, Los Angeles (UCLA)

Newspapers

Arizona Citizen
Arizona Daily Star
Arizona Republican
Chihuahua Enterprise, Chihuahua, Mexico
Diario Oficial, Mexico City
Excélsior, Mexico City

La Gaceta, Guaymas, Mexico
Los Angeles Times
Mexican Herald
New York Herald Tribune
San Francisco Chronicle
San Francisco Examiner
Tucson Daily Citizen
El Universal, Mexico City

Secondary Sources

Alzati, Servando A. *Historia de la Mexicanización de los Ferrocarriles Nacionales de México*. Mexico City, 1946.

Anderson, Rodney D. *Outcasts in their Own Land: Mexican Industrial Workers, 1906–1911*. DeKalb: Northern Illinois University Press, 1976.

Bailey, David C. *¡Viva Cristo Rey! The Cristero Rebellion and the Church-State Conflict in Mexico*. Austin: University of Texas Press, 1974.

Baz, Gustavo and Eduardo L. Gallo. *Historia del Ferrocarril Mexicano*. Mexico City: Editorial Innovación, 1980.

Benjamin, Thomas and Mark Wasserman, eds. *Provinces of the Revolution: Essays on Regional Mexican History, 1910–1929*. Albuquerque: University of New Mexico Press, 1990.

Bernstein, Marvin D. *Foreign Investment in Latin America: Cases and Attitudes*. New York: Alfred A. Knopf, 1966.

Bethell, Leslie, ed. *Mexico since Independence*. Cambridge: Cambridge University Press, 1991.

Bixler-Marquez, Dennis J. *Education on the Mexican Railways*. Border Issues and Public Policy, no. 9. El Paso: Center for Inter-American and Border Studies, University of Texas at El Paso, 1983.

Boyd, Consuelo. "Twenty Years to Nogales: The Building of the Guaymas-Nogales Railroad." *Journal of Arizona History* 22, no. 3 (Autumn 1981): 295–324.

Britton, John A. "In Defense of Revolution: American Journalists in Mexico, 1920–1929." *Journalism History* 5, no. 4 (Winter 1978–1979): 124–136.

Brown, Jonathan C. "Foreign and Native-Born Workers in Porfirian Mexico." *American Historical Review* 98, no. 3 (June 1993): 786–818.

———. *Oil and Revolution in Mexico*. Berkeley: University of California Press, 1993.

Burns, E. Bradford. *A History of Brazil*, 2nd ed. New York: Columbia University Press, 1980.

———. *The Poverty of Progress: Latin America in the Nineteenth Century*. Berkeley: University of California Press, 1980.

Butland, Gilbert J. *Latin America: A Regional Geography*, 2nd ed. New York: John Wiley & Sons, 1966.

Caballero, Romero R. Flores. *Evolución de la frontera norte*. Monterrey, México: Centro de Investigaciones Económicas, 1982.

Camín, Héctor Aguilar and Lorenzo Meyer. *In the Shadow of the Mexican Revolution: Contemporary Mexican History, 1910–1989*. Austin: University of Texas Press, 1993.

Cardoso, Fernando Henrique. *Dependency and Development in Latin America*. Berkeley: University of California Press, 1979.

Chapman, John Gresham. "Steam, Enterprise and Politics: The Building of the Veracruz–Mexico City Railway: 1837–1880." PhD diss., University of Texas at Austin, 1971.

Coatsworth, John. *Growth Against Development: The Economic Impact of Railroads in Porfirian Mexico*. DeKalb: Northern Illinois University Press, 1981.

Cooper, Herbert H. "Arizona Border Towns and the Huerta Revolution of February, March, and April 1913." Master's thesis, University of Southern California, 1941.

Cott, Kenneth. "Mexican Diplomacy and the Chinese Issue, 1876–1910," *Historical American Historical Review* 67, no. 1 (February 1987): 63–86.

Coverdale & Colpitts. *National Railways of Mexico. Report to the International Committee of Bankers on Mexico*. New York: Coverdale & Colpitts, Consulting Engineers, 1929.

Cuellar, Alfredo B. *La situación financiera de los Ferrocarriles Nacionales de México con relación al trabajo*. Mexico City: Facultad de Derecho y Ciencias Sociales, Universidad Nacional Autónoma de México, 1935.

Davis, Clarence B., Ronald E. Robinson, and Kenneth E. Wilburn Jr. *Railway Imperialism*. Westport, CT: Greenwood Press, 1991.

Deverell, William. *Railroad Crossing: Californians and the Railroad, 1850–1910*. Berkeley: University of California Press, 1994.

Dufoo, Carlos Díaz. *Limantour*. Mexico City: Eusebio Gomez de la Puente, 1910.

Edson, William D. "The National Railways of Mexico." *Railroad History* 160 (1989): 60–131.

Estatuos; Ferrocarriles Nacionales de México; Ley, decreto y escritura relativos a la constitución de la compañía. Mexico City: American Book & Printing Co., 1908.

"La Expropriacion de bienes de la empresa Ferrocarriles Nacionales de México, S.A. Mexico." *Boletín del Archivo General de la Nación* 6, no. 4 (1982): 25–34.

Facts and Figures about Mexico and Her Great Railroad: The Mexican Central. Mexico City: Bureau of Information of the Mexican Central Railway Co., 1987.

Ficker, Sandra Kuntz. *Empresa extranjera y mercado interno: El Ferrocarril Central Mexicano, 1880–1907.* Mexico City: El Colegio de México, 1995.

——. "Economic Backwardness and Firm Strategy: An American Railroad Corporation in Nineteenth-Century Mexico." *HAHR* 80, no. 2 (May 2000): 267–298.

Ficker, Sandra Kuntz and Paolo Riguzzi, eds. *Ferrocarriles y vida económica en México (1850–1950): Del surgimiento tardío al decaimiento precoz.* Mexico City: Colegio Mexiquense, 1996.

Font, Gustavo Molina. *El desastre de los Ferrocarriles Nacionales de México.* Mexico City: Biblioteca de Acción Nacional, 1940.

French, William E. *In the Path of Progress: Railroads and Moral Reform in Porfirian Mexico.* New York: Greenwood Press, 1991.

Furneaux, Robin. *The Amazon: Story of a Great River.* New York: G.P. Putnam's Sons, 1969.

Glick, Edward B. *Straddling the Isthmus of Tehuantepec.* Gainesville: University of Florida Press, 1959.

Gonzales, Michael J. "U.S. Copper Companies, the Mine Workers' Movement, and the Mexican Revolution, 1910–1920." *HAHR* 76, no. 3 (August 1996): 503–534.

González, Humberto Monteón and José Luis Trueba Lara. *Chinos y antichinos en México: Documentos para su estudio.* Guadalajara, Mexico: Gobierno de Jalisco, 1988.

Goodwin, Paul B., Jr., "The Central Argentine Railway and the Economic Development of Argentina, 1854–1881." *HAHR* 57, no. 4 (November 1977): 613–632.

Goulet, Denis. *The Uncertain Promise: Value Conflicts in Technology Transfer.* New York: IDOC/North America, 1977.

Graham, Richard, ed. *The Idea of Race in Latin America, 1870–1940.* Austin, TX: University of Austin Press, 1990.

Gurza, Jaime. *La política ferrocarrilera del gobierno.* Mexico City: Tipografía de la Oficina Impresora de Estampillas, 1911.

Haine, Edgar A. *Railways Across the Andes.* Boulder, CO: Pruett Publishing Co., 1981.

Hall, Linda B. *Oil, Banks and Politics: The United States and Postrevolutionary Mexico, 1917–1924.* Austin, TX: University of Austin Press, 1995.

Hardy, Osgood. "El Ferrocarril Sud-Pacífico." *Pacific Historical Review*, 21 (1951): 261–369.

Hart, John Mason. *Empire and Revolution: The Americans in Mexico since the Civil War.* Berkeley: University of California Press, 2002.

Hernán, Sergio Ortiz. *Los ferrocarrileros hablan.* Puebla, Mexico: Centro de Investigaciones Históricas del Movimiento Obrero, 1983.

Herzog, Lawrence A. *Changing Boundaries in the Americas: New Perspectives on the U.S.–American, Central American, and South American Borders.* San Diego: Center for U.S.–Mexican Studies, University of California at San Diego, 1992.

Hofsommer, Don L. *The Southern Pacific, 1901–1985.* College Station: Texas A&M University Press, 1986.

Hu-Dehart, Evelyn. "Development and Rural Rebellion: Pacification of the Yaquis in the Late Porfiriato." *HAHR* 54, no. 1 (February 1974): 72–93.

Kirchner, John A. and John R. Signor. *The Southern Pacific of Mexico and the West Coast Route.* San Marino, CA: Golden West Books, 1987.

Knight, Alan. *The Mexican Revolution.* Cambridge: Cambridge University Press, 1986.

——. *U.S.–Mexican Relations, 1910–1940: An Interpretation.* San Diego: Center for U.S.–Mexican Studies, University of California at San Diego, 1987.

Kolko, Gabriel. *Railroads and Regulation, 1877–1916.* Princeton, NJ: Princeton University Press, 1965.

Linder, Fred E. *The United States Railway Mission in Mexico.* Washington, D.C.: Institute of Inter-American Transportation, 1947.

Loria, Francisco. *Lo que ha sido y debe de ser la política ferrocarrilera.* Mexico City: Tipografía Económica, 1914.

——. *Los ferrocarrileros hablan.* Puebla, Mexico: Centro de Investigaciones Históricas del Movimiento Obrero, 1983.

Macedo, Pablo. *La evolución mercantil, Comunicaciones y obras públicas, La Hacienda pública: Tres monografías que dan idea de una parte de la evolución económica de México.* Mexico City: J. Bollescá, 1905.

Mancera, Gabriel. *Ferrocarril interoceánico: Discurso pronunciado por el Señor Don Gabriel Mancera . . .* Mexico City: Impr. de N. Chavez, á cargo de M. Lara hijo, 1872.

Martin, Charles E., ed. *Representative Modern Constitutions.* Los Angeles: Times-Mirror Press, 1923.

McCullough, David. *The Path between the Seas: The Creation of the Panama Canal, 1870–1914.* New York: Simon & Schuster, 1977.

McNeely, John H. *The Railways of Mexico: A Study in Nationalization.* El Paso: Texas Western College Press, 1964.

Meinig, David W. *Southwest: Three Peoples in Geographic Change, 1600–1700.* New York: Oxford University Press, 1971.

Mercer, Lloyd J. *E. H. Harriman: Master Railroader.* Boston, MA: Twayne Publishers, 1985.

Meyer, Jean A. *The Cristero Rebellion: The Mexican People between Church and State, 1926–1929.* Cambridge: Cambridge University Press, 1976.

Ministero de Comunicaciones y Obras Públicas. *Cuadros estadísticos de ferrocarriles.* Mexico City: Talleres Gráficos de la Secretaría de Comunicaciones y Obras Públicas, 1912.

Mishima, María Elena Ota. *Seite migraciones japonesas en México, 1890–1978*. Mexico City: Colegio de México, 1982.

Moncada, Carlos. *Me llamo Empalme*. Hermosillo, Mexico: Editorial Latino-americana, 1988.

Nicoli, José Patricio. *El estado de Sonora. Yaquís y Mayos: Estudio histórico*. Mexico City: Imprenta de Francisco Díaz de Leon, 1885.

O'Brien, Thomas. *The Century of U.S. Capitalism in Latin America*. Albuquerque: University of New Mexico Press, 1999.

O'Dell, Andrew C. *Railways and Geography*. London: Hutchinson University Library, 1971.

Orsi, Richard. *Sunset Limited: The Southern Pacific Railroad and the Development of the American West, 1850–1930*. Berkeley: University of California Press, 2005.

Packenham, Robert A. *The Dependency Movement: Scholarship and Politics in Development Studies*. Cambridge, MA: Harvard University Press, 1992.

Pardo, Gustavo Lopez. *La administración obrera de los Ferrocarriles Nacionales de México*. Mexico City: Universidad Nacional Autónoma de México & El Caballito, 1997.

Parlee, Lorena M. "The Impact of United States Railroad Unions on Organized Labor and Government Policy in Mexico (1880–1911)." *HAHR* 64, no. 4 (August 1984): 443–475.

Pike, Frederick B. *The United States and Latin America: Myths and Stereotypes of Civilization and Nature*. Austin: University of Texas Press, 1992.

Pletcher, David. "The Development of Railroads in Sonora." *Inter-American Economic Affairs* 1, no. 4 (1948): 3–45.

——. *Rails, Mines and Progress: Seven American Promoters in Mexico, 1867–1911*. Cornell, NY: Published for the American Historical Association [by] Cornell University Press, 1958.

Powell, Fred Wilbur. *The Railroads of Mexico*. Boston: The Stratford Co., 1921.

Price, Waterhouse & Co., *National Railways of Mexico: Report Upon Their Financial Condition*. New York: International Committee of Bankers on Mexico, 1929.

Raat, Dirk W. "Positivism in Díaz Mexico, 1876–1910: An Essay in Intellectual History." PhD diss., University of Utah, 1967.

Randall, Robert W. "Mexico's Pre-Revolutionary Reckoning with Railroads." *Américas* 42, no. 1 (July 1985): 1–28.

Roa, Fernando González. *El problema ferrocarrilero y la compañía de los Ferrocarriles Nacionales de México*. Mexico City: Carranza e Hijos, 1915.

Roman, Richard. "Railroad Nationalization and the Formation of administracion obrera in Mexico, 1937–1938." *Inter-American Economic Affairs* 35, no. 3 (1981): 3–22.

Schivelbusch, Wolfgang. *The Railway Journey: The Industrialization of Time and Space in the 19th Century.* Leamington Spa, Germany: Berg Publishers, 1986.

Smith, Peter H. *Talons of the Eagle: Dynamics of U.S.–Latin American Relations.* New York: Oxford University Press, 1996.

Spicer, Edward H. *The Yaquis: A Cultural History.* Tucson: University of Arizona Press, 1980.

Talbot, Frederick A. *The Railway Conquest of the World.* London: William Heinemann, 1911.

Thomas, Estelle Webb. *Uncertain Sanctuary: A Story of Mormon Pioneering in México.* Salt Lake City, UT: Westwater Press, 1980.

Topik, Steven. *The Political Economy of the Brazilian State, 1889-1930.* Austin: University of Texas Press, 1987.

Trennert, Robert A., Jr. "The Southern Pacific of Mexico." *Pacific Historical Review* 35 (1966): 265–284.

Tuck, Jim. *The Holy War in Los Altos: A Regional Analysis of Mexico's Cristero Rebellion.* Tucson: University of Arizona Press, 1982.

Van Hoy, Teresa M. " 'La Marcha Violenta'? Railroads and Land in Nineteenth-Century Mexico." *Bulletin of Latin American Research* 19, no. 1 (January 2000): 33–61.

Waters, L. L. *Steel Trails to Santa Fe.* Lawrence: University of Kansas Press, 1950.

Wells, Allen. "All in the Family: Railroads and Henequen Monoculture in Porfirian Yucatán." *HAHR* 72, no. 2 (May 1992): 159–210.

Whitaker, Arthur. *The Western Hemisphere Idea: Its Rise and Decline.* Ithaca, NY: Cornell University Press, 1954.

Wilson, Neill C. *Southern Pacific: The Roaring Story of a Fighting Railroad.* New York: McGraw-Hill Book Company, 1952.

Wyllys, Rufus Kay. "Sud-Pacífico: Postscript on a Railroad." *Historical Society of Southern California Quarterly* 37, no. 1 (1955): 23–32.

Yenne, Bill. *The History of the Southern Pacific.* New York: Bison Books, 1985.

Zimmerman, Gloria Leff. *Los pactos obreros y la institución presidencial en México, 1915–1938.* Azcapotzalco, México: Universidad Autónoma Metropolitana, 1991.

INDEX

ABOUT THE AUTHOR

Daniel Lewis currently serves as the full-time Dibner Senior Curator for the History of Science and Technology for the Huntington Library in Southern California, where his work includes oversight of the railroad and transportation materials. He also serves as an adjunct faculty member at Claremont Graduate University in Claremont, California, where he teaches courses on curatorial and archival theory and practice. Lewis received his PhD in Latin American History from the University of California at Riverside in 1997. He has written a wide variety of review essays, articles, and reviews on the history of science, technology, and the history of the western United States and Mexico. Most recently he co-authored *Star Struck: One Thousand Years of the Art and Science of Astronomy* (University of Washington Press, 2001). He consults widely on archival projects throughout California and is the current president of the Society of California Archivists. Lewis, a native of Hawaii, has held postdoctoral fellowships at the Smithsonian Institution, Oxford, and the Huntington Library. His current research interests concern the struggles to establish the modern scientific study of birds in the Western Hemisphere.